D1465183

THE ART OF PEACE

■

JEREMY P. TARCHER/PUTNAM

a member of Penguin Group (USA) Inc.

New York

Balance over Conflict in
Sun-tzu's The Art of War

THE ART OF PEACE

TRANSLATED AND ADAPTED BY
PHILIP DUNN

平

Page 93: Leopold Staff, from *Empty Room*, published by Dufour Editions, 1983. Pages 57–58: Dhammapada—translated and adapted by the author from a translation into Tibetan from Pali by dGe-'dun Chos-'phel.

Frontispiece: Dilip Mehta, 1996—Corbis.

Most Tarcher/Putnam books are available at special quantity discounts for bulk purchase for sales promotions, premiums, fund-raising, and educational needs. Special books or book excerpts also can be created to fit specific needs. For details, write Penguin Group (USA) Inc. Special Markets, 375 Hudson Street, New York, NY 10014.

Jeremy P. Tarcher/Putnam
a member of
Penguin Group (USA) Inc.
375 Hudson Street
New York, NY 10014
www.penguin.com

Copyright © 2003 by Philip Dunn
All rights reserved. This book, or parts thereof, may
not be reproduced in any form without permission.
Published simultaneously in Canada

Library of Congress Cataloging-in-Publication Data
Dunn, Philip, date.
The art of peace : balance over conflict in Sun-tzu's 'The art of war' /
translated and adapted by Philip Dunn.
p.   cm.
On t.p. the Chinese character of 'Ping' appears.
ISBN 1-58542-225-8
1. Sunzi, 6th cent. B.C. Sunzi bing fa.   2. Military art and science.   I. Sunzi,
6th cent. B.C. Sunzi bing fa. English.   II. Title.
UI01.S953D86   2003   2002045176
355.02—dc21

Printed in the United States of America
1   3   5   7   9   10   8   6   4   2

This book is printed on acid-free paper. ♾

BOOK DESIGN BY JENNIFER ANN DADDIO

TO MANUELA DUNN MASCETTI

平

CONTENTS

The Sutras

PEACEFUL CAMPAIGNS

THE PATHLESS PATH

FORMATION

FLEXIBILITY

CONTACT

ENERGY

平

PICTURES OF CHINA

In *The Art of Peace,* I have attempted to bring a radically new but also entirely natural perspective to the classic Chinese study, *The Art of War,* written more than two millennia ago by Sun-tzu ping-fa. *The Art of Peace* interprets this seminal text for the modern spiritual warrior in a way that I hope will bring a new vision for the human spirit, drawing a picture of our potential to guide humanity into line with an otherwise peaceful planet Earth.

The original *Art of War,* from which the translation and interpretations in this book are taken, is expressed in the Chinese written language, which is pictogramic—i.e., consisting of pictures, not words in the sense that most other languages are written. The original *Art of War* therefore was, in effect, drawn, not written. Each utterance in Chinese is made up of strokes of the brush or pen, and pictograms are in fact used as art forms as well as expressions intended to relate information.

The Chinese written language assigns a single distinctive symbol, or "character," to each word of the vocabulary. Knowledge of 2,000 to 3,000 characters is needed to read the language, and the Chinese dictionary contains more than 40,000 characters, which are arranged according to sound or form. The oldest discovered texts are oracular sayings by court diviners inscribed on tortoise shells and cattle scapulae that date from the early fourteenth century BCE, during the Shang Dynasty. These are called "oracle-bone inscriptions." Although the writing system has since been standardized and stylistically altered, its principles and many of its symbols remain fundamentally the same. The Chinese writing of today is therefore much the same picture writing used by Sun-tzu in *The Art of War* 2,500 years ago. Unlike other language scripts, however, Chinese still works pictogramically as well as phonetically. Its sound indications have not been adapted to changes of pronunciation but have remained keyed to the articulation of 3,000 years ago. The building blocks of the system are several hundred pictograms for such basic words as "man," "horse," and "axe." Expanded (or "compound") pictograms form combinations of strokes. For example, a symbol representing "man" carrying "grain" means "harvest" and also "year" (*nian*).

The content and meaning of a Chinese pictogram can

therefore vary, and may express several different concepts or notions, even an idea that may lead intrinsically to another idea, all within the one series of strokes. This provides the translator with a variety of possibilities, which very often may not be obvious, especially to us in the Western world where our language is more "single-minded." The pictogram, for example, for the word "chaos" can also mean "opportunity," depending on the context of the group of expressions on the page. Chinese seeks to inform the reader of the opportunities available within the expression and, what's more, makes us aware that there is more than one face to every situation and a story to tell in each pictogram. Perfect examples of this are the pictograms for the concepts of "war" and "peace."

The word "war" in the Chinese pictogram is a picture of a man wielding an axe and so originally may have referred to the act of cutting anything down. The pictograph 兵 for war is spoken "b'ing." The pictogram 平 for "peace" is spoken "p'ing."

The breakdown of the pictogram for peace produces a single "bamboo stem" (a left-to-right upward or horizontal stroke) or shield at the top of the pictogram, and on each end of the stroke are two short, slightly curved strokes signifying fire—fire that keeps the opposites in balance. There is also an upright stroke and crossbar beneath this, which signifies a woman safe beneath the roof of peace.

Shield and fire. The principle of "peace" in Chinese classical thought is that it forms a balance between opposing forces. When there is equilibrium between humans, then nature and the heavens are balanced and peace prevails. So you can take this word both ways—"peace" and "war"—but the Chinese believed, linguistically at least, that peace arose only through keeping humans in balance, and preferably apart, and that war arose randomly if these conditions did not prevail, at which time the axe was brought down and peace was all over. War is a random act of destruction, whereas peace is a much more complex process of sustaining through action and intelligence.

Because of the constant opportunities for "double" meanings, either as complementary opposites or as intrinsic derivations, the translator/interpreter has some flexibility in choosing which meaning to emphasize, and it was this that led the author to the realization that *The Art of War* could also be, in fact *must* be, *The Art of Peace*—for in the format of the Chinese written language, war and peace can coexist in one pictogram. The interpretations in this book, however, are not derived purely from the pictogramic aspect of the Chinese language but also from both the Tao and from Chinese and Tibetan martial arts.

The Flowing Warrior

The concept of "warrior" is not one purely involved in the battlegrounds of life the way much of modern society tends to envisage it. The ancient warrior of the Tibetan and Chinese cultures would have seen a state of chaos both as confusion and as an opportunity for change. He would have understood that the expression of war was also an expression of peace, as two constantly flowing states moving back and forth in the heart and mind. The effort of the warrior was to achieve this balance, accepting both elements of life as synchronous and flowing. This also applied to the Japanese samurai, who is depicted today in Western culture as being largely aggressive—the peaceful, honorable aspect being mostly subsumed by our warlike conditioning.

In modern Western cultures, war is the opposite of peace. Chaos is not, de facto, seen as opportunity—though with further explanation, we might understand that in a state of chaos, opportunity could arise. In the Chinese pictogram, the two derivations are taken entirely for granted and require no explanation at all, one flowing into the other and back again as a constant motion of life. In effect, therefore, we may see life expressed in this form as a verb, not a noun—movement being everything. This comprehension changes the mind of the reader, indeed the entire culture.

We can use the methods intrinsic to the so-called martial art of Tai Chi Chuan as an example to help us see the physical potential for the coexistence of aggression and peace. Note that Tai Chi in our social environment is generally lumped together with all other such forms—kung fu, aikido, jujitsu—as a "martial" art. The word "martial" conjures up implications of conflict. Above all else, Tai Chi in its original format was intended not to be conflictual per se, but as a method of dealing with conflict with a minimum of violence.

The "form" of Tai Chi—i.e., its movements—grew originally from imitating the movements of a newborn baby as it grasps the air with its hands and legs after birth—not a movement we could apply to war. Its earlier form was called "Chou-lyn" and was actually intended to ground the adept into a state of meditation and centeredness and was based on the movement of animals. The body is rooted into the earth, and the *chi* (energy) grows more and more powerful, through constant practice, into an energetic focus that arises from the belly and eventually fills the whole human frame in such a way that the warrior is both connected to the ground and merged internally, physically, psychologically, and spiritually—i.e., he is self-aware.

Tai Chi and Chou-lyn are not attack formats or even truly self-defense formats, though under certain circumstances they can be employed in either way.

Chou-lyn was originally intended to provide the warrior with self-possession, internal power, physical health, spiritual awareness, and, therefore, compassion. All the movements of the form develop these features, both inwardly and outwardly. An imbalance of aggression—i.e., too much emphasis on the "thrust" movements of the form—will actually weaken the *chi*, while too much emphasis on the "rest" movements will do the same. The process of Chou-lyn form is to keep the balance flowing between the two at all times.

This is the essence of the peaceful warrior—immensely powerful, centered, physically healthy, and, therefore, psychologically and spiritually healthy also. Essentially, the peaceful warrior flows constantly between strength and weakness, potential and withdrawal. The aggressive warrior, by contrast, is constantly putting out an energy that weakens him, draining the essential *chi* from the body. This takes place on all levels—the physical energy, the psychology, i.e., those actions in the mind engendered by conditioning that encourage aggressive thinking. Subsequently, the inner spiritual and moral well-being has little opportunity to grow because there is minimal flow between the polarities of existence. Methods used to educate the modern soldier, for example, actually produce less real power because little consideration is given to the balance that the body and mind need between strength and weakness.

On the subtlest level, the peaceful warrior learns that truth arises from inner awareness: The heart knows but does not speak, while the mind speaks but does not know.

Balancing War and Peace

The comprehension intrinsic to a language that is essentially enigmatic, such as Chinese, is not drawn simply from the language itself, but from the very basis of the entire culture that gave birth to it—a culture responsible for the pictogram and for the concept of the flow of *chi*. Most ancient civilizations, including that of China, contained intrinsic methods of demonstrating the presence of the aggressive and peaceful warrior as two aspects of a balance in society—not two opposites. One of the most common devices through which to achieve this symmetry was mythology. In the Navajo creation myths, for example, "Changing Woman" gave birth first to a boy while bathing in a spring with the sun shining upon her. She then returned and gave birth to a second boy under the light of the moon. The boy born of the sun is called "Killer of Enemies." He is the aggressive warrior, outwardly directed. The boy born of the moon is known as "Child of the Water" and becomes the medicine man, the shaman, who is inwardly directed and magical. These are seen not as opposites but as complementary twins born of the same source.

Throughout ancient civilizations such as Babylon and China—even in the Bible in the story of Moses and Aaron—the king is almost invariably twinned with the sage or magician (one who seeks solutions through inner self-knowledge), the "Merlin," so to speak. In medieval Europe, the sage is usually present beside the mythical "Arthur." It is only in our more recent "technological," industrial cultures that the "king" stands alone as the fighter and protector—the moral disciplinarian—without the aid of the sage, now departed due to social adherence to the rationality of technology. In the United States, for example, the president is partnered by one who *seeks* war—the general or admiral. The peacemaker is nowhere to be found. Joseph Campbell calls this partnering between the outer and the inner the "twin-hero" in mythology—war and peace constantly represented as two sides of the same coin. Again, the flow between the two sides of life is needed to sustain a balanced society.

In ancient China, the balance was kept throughout the culture—in mythology, within the royal court, and even in the language itself. Sun-tzu, being a Taoist, was positioned to advise the emperor on matters of peaceful coexistence. The whole purpose of the Tao is to express the flowing nature and the enigmatic essence of the Way.

Finding Our Own Balance

All this lies within Sun-tzu's pictograms of the original *Art of War*—flowing like the form of Tai Chi between positive and negative, power and weakness, joy and sadness, and supported by the presence of the emperor's power and the magician's (in this case, Sun-tzu's) inner understanding—intuition, instinct, etc.

To illustrate the contrasts available in Sun-tzu, the following translations/interpretations can be seen to arise from the same set of pictograms.

The aggressive meaning:

War is the art of deception (bringing down)—appear to be strong when you are weak, appear to be far away when you are near, appear to be inept when you are able.

The peaceful meaning:

Peace is the art of inception (raising up)—allow strength and weakness, accept poise and vulnerability both, face death and suffer pain.

In the aggressive interpretation, the Western mind draws upon the seemingly intrinsic implication that in order to succeed we must first be determined to win. This is prioritized; in fact, it is the very basis for our whole way of life. Therefore, if we view life as an aggressive challenge, we must essentially lie about our condition (for life cannot be otherwise controlled)—deceive the opponent by displaying false information and therefore fool him into a position whereby we may defeat him. This in turn arises from a lack of self-awareness and self-acceptance, possibly the biggest frailty from which modern Westernized humanity suffers—the debility of not knowing or accepting our own weaknesses and therefore never meeting the magician in us.

In the second interpretation, the same conditions are essentially present, but they are based on something positive and "inceptive"—i.e., honesty and self-awareness. Here also is the implication that life is not *a priori* a battle. I allow both sides of my nature to be available—strength and weakness—not denying one or the other but flowing between them. I accept that I am both strong *and* weak, private (poised) *and* sensitive. I am willing to concur with existence to the extent of facing death and suffering from life—both. The two interpretations produce utterly different results, intrinsically, and intrinsic to the same original text—the same set of pictograms—from the same mind, and the same culture. The choice is ours to make.

It is not merely, of course, the presence of the different language that results in a broader and more complex awareness. *The Art of Peace* is a new way of looking at conflict and a starting point on the journey of self-discovery that ultimately must lead to a more peaceful society. The awareness that is gained from inner discovery leads us to realize that what previously appeared to be in conflict is in reality complementary—one and the same.

Only self-awareness and consciousness cause this one-and-the-sameness to adhere. Without consciousness, the opposites continue to tug at each other, and the potential for conflict overwhelms the potential for peaceful coexistence. Thus the suffering. As displayed on a California bumper sticker, "You can't make peace at the same time as preparing for war!"

In this constant and habitual belief that we exist solely as part of a quest to win, we essentially lose. We lose the delicate balance of nature, our own health, and the price-less and irreplaceable wealth of awareness.

From our twenty-first-century perspective, we attempt to *make* peace, as though this were possible, employing external processes such as manipulation, craft, and might rather than the affirming and accepting power that arises out of contemplation and inner silence. Peace in this sense amounts only to a brittle control prone to failure at any time. Look at any political imbalance in troubled locations. At one time or another during the twentieth century, more than half the world was either at war or on the edge of war.

Peace in this century is still *made* out of the control achieved through successful war, the threat of war, or a strategy to prevent it, and therefore will inevitably result in war again because control from an unbalanced nature cannot be maintained.

Much of modern Western religion together with our belief that we can control life play a great part in this determination to create conflict amongst ourselves.

The great Zen philosopher Daisetz Suzuki once gave a talk in Ascona, Switzerland, his first talk in that country. The audience was made up of Europeans, and they sat looking at this tiny Japanese man before them. He was ninety-one years old at the time, and, looking straight at the audience, he said, "Nature against God. God against Nature. Nature against Man. Man against Nature. Man against God. God against Man. Very funny religion." It is the traditional doctrine of the Fall that provides us with this idea—that the world is not to be accepted and affirmed as it is; it must, in our minds, be corrected.

There is no peace in this.

There can be no balance in our hearts where even nature is under attack, where there is no acknowledgment of the co-incidence of her positive and negative powers.

The Art of Peace, therefore, is designed to bring this fundamental misunderstanding of the balances in life and nature to light and to afford the twenty-first-century reader an ancient, time-tested method for achieving peace.

A translation and interpretation of the greater majority of the original sutras have been included. Those that have been excluded are the very few that constitute detailed commentary on previous sutras.

The Sutras

CONFLICT

AND PEACE

[1]

■

Conflict and peaceful coexistence are central aspects of life—indeed they are the basis for survival—and bring both destruction and creativity. We must therefore examine them closely.

Just to reiterate what was mentioned in the introduction, the movements of Tai Chi grew originally from imitating those of a newborn baby as it grasps the air with its hands and legs after birth. These are not movements we could apply to war. Its earlier generic form was called "Chou-lyn," which included 36 different applications, all of which were intended to ground the adept into a state of meditation and centeredness and were based on the movements of animals. The body is rooted into the earth, and the *chi* (energy) grows more and more powerful, through constant practice, into an energetic broad focus that arises from the belly, the *hara,* and eventually fills the whole human frame so that the warrior is both connected to the ground and merged internally, physically, psychologically, and spiritually, thus becoming self-aware. Chou-lyn is not an attack format nor even truly a self-defense format, though under certain circumstances some parts of the different applications can be employed in either way.

Chou-lyn was originally intended to provide the warrior with self-possession, internal power, physical health, spiritual awareness, and, therefore, compassion. All the movements of the different forms develop these features, both inwardly and outwardly. An imbalance of aggression—i.e., too much emphasis on the "thrust" movements of the form—will actually weaken the *chi,* while too much emphasis on the "rest" movements will do the same. The process of Chou-lyn forms is to keep the balance flowing between the two at all times.

This is the essence of the peaceful warrior—immensely powerful, centered, physically healthy, and, therefore, psychologically and spiritually healthy also. Essentially, the peaceful warrior flows constantly between strength and weakness, potential and withdrawal. The aggressive warrior, by contrast, is constantly putting out an energy that weakens him, draining the essential *chi* from the body. This takes place on all levels—the physical energy, the psychology, i.e., those actions in the mind engendered by conditioning that encourage aggressive thinking. Subsequently, the inner spiritual and moral well-being has little opportunity to grow because there is minimal flow between the polarities of existence. Methods used to educate the modern soldier, for example, actually produce less real power because little consideration is given to the balance that the body and mind need between strength and weakness.

On the subtlest level, the peaceful warrior learns that truth arises from inner awareness—the heart knows but does not speak, while the mind speaks but does not know.

Each of us holds both conflict and creativity as natural forces within us. We need both to survive and to enjoy life. But if we live completely as survivors—warlike and aggressive—we lead unbalanced lives, and imbalance brings suffering to all of us and the world we live in. A life well lived is not a matter of being creative *or* destructive, but of flowing back and forth between the two. A joyful life exists in that flow, rather than in the extremes that lie at each end of it. Like the Chou-lyn adept's *chi* energy, we must accept our natural flow among all elements of life—from strength to weakness, from love to hate, from doubt to certainty, from *conflict* to *peaceful coexistence* . . . Awareness, which brings relaxation and therefore peace, lies in the flow itself. Awareness, and therefore peace, is clouded at either extreme, whereas the benefits of consciousness become fully available to us when we flow along the middle path, never tarrying in one extreme or the other.

Look into your most intimate relationships. Do you always love the person closest to you? The problem arises only when you do not want to be angry or jealous but want always to love—when you deny the negative. The truth is that you flow between emotions constantly—love, anger, love, doubt. This is your nature; accept it, and the relaxation that results will bring power and self-awareness because as you watch the flow, so it becomes familiar, and you begin to understand your nature *as it is* rather than as you would wish it to be.

Peaceful coexistence is not a matter of holding on to a constant state of creativity and peace. You cannot "hold on" to peace. Peace exists when you accept the flow of change. If your life has been largely one of pressure and difficulty, you will yearn for creativity and silence. This yearning will not help you to be creative or silent but will instead bring more pressure upon you. What you need is inner awareness—the knowledge of what is actually happening and then the acceptance of it, whatever it is. This will bring enormous energy and power.

However, flowing in the middle way is not a repression

of extremes. In indicating the path, we are not forbidding the many fields that lie on either side of it. It is only that the fields of joy and suffering appear different when we are easy and relaxed in the middle way of conscious awareness. The flowers are as visible as the thorns when you are not buried amongst them.

[2]

■

Study the art of peace according to five crucial matters—the Tao (love), heaven on earth (consciousness), vigilance, silence, power. Develop methods using these five matters to be responsive to all events.

These five basic tenets are the ground of all being. The rest of the work is founded upon them. Without understanding these, we won't find inner peace and we won't be able to project a balanced existence to the rest of the world.

Develop methods using these five matters to be responsive to all events.

The Tao (Love)

The Tao, or the Way, may be seen here as love. This presence is like a lake in which we all bathe, generated by life for our benefit. We are bathing constantly in this lake, but we may not always be aware of the benefits it gives us. The Way is relaxation that ends all conflict. Relaxation arises out of self-acceptance—accept that you are sad, accept that you are happy, accept that you hate, accept that you cannot accept. If I know and love who I am, I may know and love who you are. In Taoist terms, the Way is that which cannot be described. The best way to exemplify this is by using an old Taoist story.

A master who lived as a hermit on a mountain was asked by a monk, "What is the Way?"

The master answered, "What a fine mountain this is."

The monk was asking about the Way, and the master was telling him how fine the mountain is. A strange response.

If the master had told the monk something relevant, he would not have helped him. The monk was the problem, and if the master had spoken with relevance, it would have meant he had adjusted to the monk.

This gap between the question and the answer can be bridged only if the disciple has trust. So how do we bridge the gap between the seeker and the master, between the question and the answer?

In this, trust becomes the most significant thing, not knowledge, or logic, or argument. A deep trust bridges the irrelevant answer—a trust that can see through the irrelevance and catch a glimpse of the relevance.

"What a fine mountain this is," the master said in reply.

"I am not asking you about the mountain," said the monk, "but the Way."

The master replied, "So long as you cannot go beyond the mountain, my son, you cannot reach the Way."

Heaven on Earth
(Consciousness or Awareness)

The question here is: How do we become more conscious, more aware of heaven on earth? Consciousness is not something to be achieved, but a presence that is available. Consciousness arises only out of awareness of that presence. Awareness of that presence arises only when we are in balance. Balance arises only when we accept who we are within the flow or *chi* of our lives.

In Chinese medicine, which works through the balancing of the *chi*, the fundamental requirement is the flow of that *chi*, or energy, though there is no urgency about it. The flow of the *chi* arises from an inner balance and thereby heals us constantly, making us conscious also.

Lao-tzu, who exemplified the original Tao, emphasized

that the principle underlying inner silence, and therefore the availability of conscious awareness, is that force defeats itself. Every action produces a reaction, every challenge a response. There is a tendency for every aspect of this existence to continue to be what it is. Interfere with its natural state and it resists, as a stone resists crushing. If it is a living creature, it resists actively, as a wasp being crushed will sting. In human beings, this tendency is particularly advanced and unique, and the ultimate result of more and more action is likely to be more and more resistance (such as modern warfare); therefore, we discover the opposite of what was intended.

Conscious awareness is not intended, but it is available.

Vigilance

The mind follows what the heart sustains. It is the voice of the heart that knows the truth of what we actually need. The mind is servant to the heart, following its instructions when they are clear. The more self-aware we become, listening deeper and deeper within ourselves, the better we learn what we actually need—the better clarity we learn.

The inner desire of the heart is sustaining, as it arises

out of a genuine understanding of life. The mind then follows with plans for fulfillment. This is vigilance, another aspect of conscious awareness. Like everything else related to consciousness, it requires practice and familiarity.

Silence

Silence rewards, provides, bathes. The Earth is silent, and in the context of the original Sun-tzu notion, it is our guide. Merge with the world and be silent.

Silence is a gift to ourselves. It is like a reward for good deeds. Noise saps us of our energy. Silence brings that energy back, and it must be encouraged. Find ways to be silent; there are many of them. Go to a silent place such as a mountain or a park or a church where there are few people. Sit in an empty space alone, and listen to the silence inside you.

Power

Power is not physical or mental. It is a lack of blame. It arises out of the existence of the other four crucial matters—love, consciousness, vigilance, and silence. Find these four, and power comes naturally to you, emanating from your innermost being.

Real power is not the ability to manipulate yourself or others; it is the personal power to be responsible for your own life. If you are truly responsible, leveling no blame against others, then you will be powerful. If you blame others for your condition, you are weak, for you have relinquished the ability to move your own life. If you accept responsibility for everything you do, you can change it. Thus personal power arises. In this sense, you have the same responsibilities as God, and therefore the same power.

Here is an old Hindu story, to exemplify how we constantly put blame on others to no effect. A man driving his car on a lonely road suspected that he had missed the path and was moving in the wrong direction. He saw a beggar walking by, so he stopped the car and asked the beggar, "Does this road lead to Delhi?"

The beggar said, "I don't know."

So the man asked, "Does this road lead to Agra?"

The beggar said, "I don't know."

The man became very irritated and said to the beggar angrily, "So you don't know much."

The beggar laughed and said, "But I am not lost."

THE WAY

[3]

■

The Way means living with all humanity in a fundamental understanding so that no one will fear life or death, making danger insignificant.

Be aware of the Way. Those that know it will be joyful. Those that do not know it will not be joyful.

Fear is the biggest problem of human life. If we are unaware and unaccepting of the inner aspect of ourselves, then we are bound to be frightened, because we have no ground to stand on. It's like trying to plant a tree in water. The tree is not used to having so much water around it. How will it grow if it cannot even stand? How will it get food if there is no earth for it to put down roots? Without self-knowledge, we are like the tree floating on water, tossed and turned at the whim of the river.

This is the basis for all prejudice. Lack of self-knowledge leads inevitably to lack of knowledge of others.

Prejudice is hate born of fear, which is born of ignorance of the self. If I know and love my own weakness, how can I not be compassionate about the weaknesses of others?

Here is another wonderful tale, drawn from medieval Europe, that exemplifies the rewards of loving our own weaknesses and losing our prejudices as a result.

It is said that a French prince visited a jail. In honor of the royal guest, the prison warden offered to release any prisoner the prince might designate. To pick out that prisoner, the prince began interviewing each of the men privately, asking, "Why are you here?"

"I'm innocent, my lord!" cried one.

"I've been framed!" pleaded another.

Perjury, prejudice, injustice, and oppression were reasons given by the convicts for their imprisonment.

Only one man told a different story. "Your highness," he replied, "I deserve to be here, and I have no complaint. In my time, I have been a wicked, desperate murderer. It is a great mercy, both to society and to myself, that I am here."

"You wicked wretch!" the prince replied. "What a pity you should be confined among so many honest citizens. You admit yourself that you are evil enough to corrupt them all. I can't allow you to remain in their company another day. Guard! This is the man I wish released!"

[4]

■

Therefore, employ the five crucial matters to discover the best conditions. More precisely: Which is the best method to comprehend the Way? Which inner and outer conditions will stand firm? Which methods are most effective for learning? What environment will provide the best conditions? What are the ways for self-satisfaction? This is how you can know the ways that will bring results.

Approach everything through generosity and concern, conscious awareness, strength and clarity of vision, silence, and personal power—the five crucial matters. Stand firm in these, and the outside will appear clearly.

Discover first what your true needs are in each circumstance that you face. Perhaps you are looking for new work—listen to what you would prefer to do rather than what you believe to be the only work you could get. Broaden your outlook to fit with your personal needs—

financial, environmental, and creative. Get as close to the ideal as possible.

Joseph Campbell called this "following your bliss."

Work toward something lasting and fruitful, and do not be afraid to change your circumstances.

Consider the outside possibilities according to your inner needs: Do I want real wealth (i.e., not just financial)? Do I want to love and be loved? Do I want to live in a home that enhances my life? Do I want to be healthy and unstressed, or do I prefer to be working under stress and pressure?

These questions, if they arise from a clear heart, will quickly be answered, and circumstances will arise for self-satisfaction.

[5]

■

Assess the advantage of taking advice, and structure your inner and outer work accordingly, to provide extra-ordinary methods. Methods should be structured with wisdom, imagination, and order, based on what will most effectively coincide with the Way.

The first question is: Do you need advice or help from outside yourself? Perhaps your own resources are not adequate. Will support from someone or something else enhance your own comprehension and help produce an extra-ordinary result? Do not think yourself an island. You are part of the world around you. Once again, examine the need for advice from a clear heart.

Methods should be structured with wisdom, imagination, and order, based on what will most effectively coincide with the Way.

Remember the five crucial matters. Before approaching something important, stop. Consider in silence; listen to your heart rather than the confusion engendered in the mind. The ability to be still when surrounded by confusion is no more than a new habit that can be gained with practice.

Listen first to your inner self, and then make the decisions out of that wisdom, imagination (daring), and order. Inner wisdom is achieved by flowing in the middle Way, imagination is there to allow you breadth of opportunity, and order is needed to keep your life simple and healthy and to preserve energy.

[6]

∎

Peace is the art of inception (raising up)—allow strength and weakness, accept poise and vulnerability both, face death and suffer pain.

Inception is the opposite of deception. "Deception," in its original derivation, means "bringing down," while "inception" means "raising up."

We are often afraid that if we open ourselves to others by being honest, we become vulnerable or open to attack. It is therefore difficult to be honest with ourselves, for we fear that in a state of weakness we will be taken advantage of and hurt or that others will not approve of who we are. This is because we ourselves do not know who we are.

Once we become relaxed into self-knowledge, inner truth is natural and simple and requires no defending. If I can say "I am what I am" and accept it as the foundation for life, vulnerability and strength become a joy as two sides of the same coin. There is nothing to prove to ourselves or to anyone else.

Saint Teresa of Avila said, "Heaven exists all the way to heaven—I am the way, the truth, and the light." This is not a religious statement but a therapeutic one—truth cures along the way to heaven (light).

Remember that the energy of the *chi* flows *between* strength and weakness, never remaining one or the other— like a river between banks, flowing over boulders and around trees, in constant flux. This reflects life, for we *are* weak and vulnerable, and we *do* suffer and eventually die. The truth lies in the facts. Hiding it by always wishing to be strong and impregnable merely emphasizes the opposites. Learn who you are, and take joy from it always. Everything else follows.

[7]

∎

When applying wisdom, never be obvious, but be playful and flexible. When you are approaching the problem from nearby, make your move from far away. When you approach from far away, make your move from nearby. Inceptive confusion is constructive and entertaining. Be daring and unpredictable.

This sutra is about being good-natured and supple with the problems in your life. We normally approach difficult situations through habitual methods. If we have a problem, the usual way is to worry and to contemplate becoming more serious in the future to overcome the problem. This method only increases stress and anxiety and causes us to concentrate our efforts more intensely, thereby making the problems worse. There is another way.

When you are approaching the problem from nearby, make your move from far away.

The closer the problem is to you, the more you will identify with it, and therefore the blinder you will be to broader solutions. Step back. Contemplate in silence without searching for answers. Apply the five crucial matters—self-concern, conscious awareness, strength and clarity of vision, silence, and personal power. Be with yourself, breathe gently, and allow the specific to evaporate. Identification with the problem will disperse into a wider vision, and results will be easier to discover.

Inceptive confusion is constructive and entertaining. Be daring and unpredictable.

Once you have disengaged from the problem and feel calmer about it, allow yourself to be a little unpredictable—take risks. Perhaps the condition requires a little imagination. Perhaps it can be alleviated by using a different approach. By stepping back from it, other alternative perspectives become available almost as if by magic. Stand too close to a tree, and you will not see the way through the forest.

Conversely—*When you approach from far away, make your move from nearby.*

Where the problem arises far away from you, you need to come closer to it to find a solution. Once again, apply the five crucial matters. Do not panic through lack of information. The solution may become entirely obvious once you know the facts. Be intimate with the conditions that you face. Knowledge and understanding disperse fear. You cannot learn how to climb a tree if you are standing far from the forest. And here, too, once you have discovered details of the situation, be daring. Use your imagination for finding interesting and flexible solutions.

By creating a new formula in the face of a habitual condition, you will provide yourself with a method that can be used again and again in the future.

[8]

■

Do not structure your personal campaigns precisely, though be aware of their shape. Make your efforts adaptable and off-guard. Do not speak of your plans to others, for your being will be at its best in silence and privacy. Others can have only opinions, and opinions are also private.

When you choose to adjust some aspect of your regular behavior—such as diet, physical health, or an old habit—do not be rigid in the way you go about it. Strictness does not bring good results, for your body is not a stone temple; otherwise, you would not need the tender vessels of eyes and ears, feelings and sensitivity. Rather, listen and watch for all processes within yourself and adapt your campaigns accordingly. The more aware you are of your changing inner needs, the better the results of your campaigns. Remember that you are made of constantly flowing energy, ever fluctuating.

Do not become guarded against failure, for this brings only tension. Be conscious of influences and their impact on your moment-to-moment responses. Sometimes you will be tired; adjust to this. Other times you will have great strength; adjust to this. Remain vigilant, however, in your intentions for change. To be vigilant is not to be hard or conservative but to be flexible and free, nevertheless remaining intimately in touch with who you are at all times.

Also, keeping your positive inner life private from others will allow it to be flexible and tenderhearted. It is yours alone and deserves the utmost care. Others will have private agendas that they may wish to impose upon you. The inner life of others is as unique and private to them as yours is to you, though they may not be aware of this and may wish, therefore, to influence your behavior.

When you listen to all opinions, you become fragmented. When you are whole, you are holy.

This sutra applies very much to the influences of advertising and social awareness. Dieting is but one example of how we are all influenced by the outside and are therefore very often unable to listen to what is happening inside us and our actual needs—which are always unique to each of us.

Most diets fail to achieve the result we want because they are generalized out of the desire of the diet-maker to benefit financially, whereas if we comprehend our own body and habits we can most easily manage the "campaign" successfully. In addition to this, there is a different tendency amongst different social environments. Eating too much is neurotic. Fasting is the opposite neurosis, but still neurotic. What we should all do is eat as much as is needed by the body, without ever eating too much. But this isn't how it works, because we are subject to so many stresses and strains, and food is a palliative. Whenever a society becomes very rich, fasting or dieting becomes a cult.

In India, the Jaina sect is one of the richest groups—fasting is their most important determination, almost like a religion. America is rich—dieting is a fashion, even an obsession. It is difficult to find a woman who is not on a diet. People go to nature-cure clinics to fast.

A poor man's religion is always of festivity—feast. Mohammedans—often poor people—feast on religious holidays. They starve the whole year round, but for the religious holiday, at least on that day, they change their clothes and enjoy one day of feasting.

Jains feast the whole year, and when their religious days come, they fast. A poor man's festival is going to be a feast; a rich man's festival is going to be a fast. People move to the opposite extreme. Find your own way, separate from your society.

[9]

■

Enter your process positively. Expect always the best of yourself and of those around you. The one who expects failure before starting will find failure at the end. Maintain all skills and abilities favorably. The one who expects to forget before starting will forget at the end.

Watching others in this way, you can see who is relaxed and loving, and those who need help.

Remain willing and open to everything that you undertake—this carries its own power and will be reflected back to you by existence. Regardless of judgmental voices inside your head or the opinions of others, keep in the forefront of your consciousness the fact that you are a child of life and therefore acceptable to life as you are. Expectations of failure in any activity will also be reflected back by existence, for the universe does not judge—it merely supplies what is prayed for. Sustain your abilities, skills, and positive understanding with a nurturing regard, caring for the vulnerable being that lives within you. If you forget who you are, existence will also forget, and your vigilance will have no ground to stand on.

Mastering this self-regard and positive embracing of life, you will also discover compassion for others.

PEACEFUL
CAMPAIGNS

[10]

∎

Do not undertake long personal campaigns, or through inner exhaustion future campaigns will fail. Be aware that reducing the needs of the body is depriving the familiar; therefore, be vigilant but tender. Keep your campaigns tenderly short but strong. Make peace with yourself through vigilance and love—these bring confidence. This way, you enjoy every campaign, even if you fail. Never fight with yourself; there is no one to win. Accept your condition until you discard it.

In your efforts to adjust aspects of your habitual behavior—through overenthusiasm or great determination—do not fight with yourself as though there were something to win, as though you were a desperate general at the head of an army who must win a war. You will always fail at war, for no war has ever been won in truth. Striving too hard or too long at physical health, for example, brings exhaustion on levels you may not be aware of, levels that will record their discomfort in ways you will not hear until next time you make further attempts, or some time later. The body will always show you its suffering, but if you are not listening, the body will echo these messages louder and louder until you hear—by which time illness may result.

Be aware that in reducing the needs of the body—through diet or exercise or psychological change—you are also depriving it of familiar habits. Depriving the familiar is hard for the body, though it will willingly adjust at its own pace. Treat it with care, and listen to the signals it gives you—aches, pains, change of breathing, change of heartbeat, lack of passion. There are many messages.

Therefore, work on yourself with strength but in short measure. Work and watch, work and watch. Be your own best friend, for this will give you confidence.

This way, winning or losing becomes irrelevant because you are enjoying the work close to someone you love—yourself.

Accept your condition until you discard it. And when the change has been made, when you have found a better way, discarding the old will happen without pain. The best friend becomes an old friend, and the habit is allowed to die peacefully.

[11]

∎

In peaceful campaigns, self-awareness and inner consciousness preserve the spirit rather than deplete it. As the spirit is preserved and respected so also is the heart. As the heart is preserved and kept healthy so is the body. As the body is preserved and respected so is the mind.

The peaceful warrior learns first about himself. Before all else, self-knowledge must be found, for this brings an appreciation of sensitivity and vulnerability. When you know yourself, you are automatically sensitive and vulnerable—there is no other way. When you do not know yourself, you are insensitive and are living in the false belief of invulnerability—an entirely unnatural state that sooner or later brings conflict, disease, and pain.

Learning this leads to consciousness, and the arrival of consciousness brings vulnerability as its partner. It is like a computer processor that requires software to function.

Without the software, the processor cannot do its job. Without consciousness, vulnerability is just painful because it functions without an understanding and compassionate environment.

Whenever you think something about somebody else—perhaps a negative judgment or opinion that arises from some prejudice—watch carefully. Look within. The cause is very likely inside you. But you don't know yourself, so you go on confusing your own projections with outer realities. It is impossible to know anything real unless you have known yourself. And the only way to know yourself is to live a life of vulnerability and openness to possibilities. Don't live in a closed cell. Don't hide yourself behind your mind. Come out.

Once you come out, you will become aware of many things inside you that were not visible before. You are not a one-room apartment; you have many rooms in a big house. But you have become used to living on the porch and have forgotten the rooms inside the house. Many rooms and surprises are hidden inside you, and those treasures constantly go on inviting you to take a look. But until you reach self-knowledge, you will be blind and deaf to them.

THE PATHLESS

PATH

[12]

∎

There is no one to conquer, and nothing to achieve. Pathways and quests bring only dissatisfaction. You are here now, like it or not. All quests and battles are therefore rendered worthless.

We tend to believe that life is a series of quests or pathways—that somehow we have to get from here to there, from birth to death, from failure to success, from the bottom of the ladder to the top. We are taught that this striving is good for us and that it will make our lives rich and comfortable. But this is what also brings personal anxiety, pain, and global conflict. This is not to say that there isn't a temporal path, but it is an illusion of the mind only and therefore of little help in the spiritual world that we are now entering.

In the same way, the religious teacher will often tell us that if we follow "this" method—praying, worshiping, meditating—we will achieve nirvana, heaven, enlightenment. We see this as a pathway along which we must travel. We believe in the raising of consciousness through pathways or methods. Words like "growth" and "improvement" are commonly used, and these translate in our minds into seeing everything as a progress toward a goal. There is no goal in the present moment because there is nothing beyond the present moment.

The peaceful warrior accepts the present as it is, and thereby changes. J. Krishnamurti, and many other masters, called this "the pathless path." In truth, there is no path, only an awareness that changes a life oriented toward goals into a life oriented by the presence of life itself. The journey is in fact the destination.

A small section from *Through the Looking Glass*, by Lewis Carroll, exemplifies the idea of any battle taking place with the self, any quest to win or succeed in any spiritual or psychological quest—any life that lives outside the present. The White Queen offers Alice jam, but Alice says she doesn't care for jam . . .

> *"It's very good jam," said the Queen.*
> *"Well, I don't want any today, at any rate."*
> *"You couldn't have it if you did want it," the Queen said.*

"The rule is, jam tomorrow and jam yesterday—but never jam today."

"It must come sometimes to 'jam today,'" Alice objected.

"No, it can't," said the Queen. "It's jam every other day: today isn't any other day, you know."

FORMATION

[13]

■

In ancient times, peaceful warriors first comprehended and practiced inner peace and then respected the vulnerability in themselves and in others; thus, there is no conflict when consciousness arises.

The fundamental problem with facing conflict lies within each of us as individuals. If we are taught to be in conflict internally, then our view of those around us will immediately be one of potential conflict.

If we learn as children and young adults to be at peace with ourselves, then our view of those around us will be compassionate and concerned, and the recognition of conflict in others will not impinge upon us. We will therefore seek to heal rather than to hurt the other.

Teaching the young to be at peace is a simple matter of teaching them to comprehend who they are. If you know who you are, you give permission to yourself to be happy.

You choose each day the path of joy rather than the path of suffering. The organized religions all teach that suffering is an essential aspect of life and that we will only be happy after life. This is a false understanding drawn from the need in early times to control society. Make people unhappy and they will obey the laws. Church and State made an agreement to enforce this basic concept on society. It is still being used as a method of control in many countries where the rulers cause women to suffer in order to control the whole society.

Hinduism works in this way also, particularly in India, where women are "owned" by men and forced into obedience through fear of death. This method is a complete bastardization of holy scriptures (the Koran, the Upanishads, etc.); men use the words of the great religious teachers for their own unenlightened ends. No scripture ever taught such things.

Teach the child to love and understand him- or herself, and all of life will change for the better throughout the world. It is the simplest doctrine in existence but the most difficult for modern humans to learn because the great majority of humans do not know who they are. The result is that we all look outward for our wisdom—toward God, toward money, and therefore always toward only war.

Don't tell the child that only God knows the answer, because God doesn't know the answer. God is only a reflection of us.

There is a wonderful story about one of the very first enlightened women in our history. Her name was Gargi, and she lived about 5,000 years ago in India at the time when the Upanishads were being written—a time when women were not yet treated as cruelly as they are now.

The story goes that at that time there was an annual contest to determine the individual of the greatest wisdom in the kingdom, and the prize was 1,000 cows, each one adorned with golden horns and studded in jewels. It was a great prize. There was one man who had often won the prize before, and his arrogance convinced him that he would win, to such an extent that he had the 1,000 gold and jeweled cows moved to his home in advance of the contest—such was his brilliance and hubris.

But Gargi came to the town center to find her husband and learned by chance of the contest and of the fact that this man, Yagnavalkya, had already assumed his victory. She went to the emperor and said that she would finish the contest with two questions to Yagnavalkya. Though the contest had never had a woman winner, the emperor agreed.

Gargi stood before Yagnavalkya and asked the first

question: "Who created the world?" Yagnavalkya answered immediately, his face smirking with derision: "Why God, of course. Everything that exists must have a creator."

Gargi smiled back and asked the second question: "Who created God, then? If everything must have a creator, who created God?"

She won the gold-horned cows, and Yagnavalkya never entered the contest again.

Why do we teach our children that God created everything?

[14]

■

Power and vulnerability are both within you and within the other.
Therefore, skillful and peaceful warriors are able to be both powerful and
vulnerable, though they have no desire to make others vulnerable. Power
can be discerned but not manufactured and is a matter of self-awareness,
while vulnerability is a matter of acceptance.

It is not that you can "achieve" power and vulnerability. Power results from being responsible for your own life—how can you be responsible for your own life if you do not know who you are? Know yourself through constant awareness, and you will become powerful.

Vulnerability also lies within you—it cannot be achieved, as it is already available. Simply see it—taste the flavor of your own heart, and you will recognize it. There are many ways to cover our vulnerability: greed for wealth, alcohol and drugs, anger and frustration—these are all attempts to hide who we are from ourselves and others. The need to hide our vulnerability is no more than our anticipation of pain because of our experiences in the past. Come to the present and let go of the camouflage, and the magical result will convince you. With the awareness of weakness comes immense strength also, for weakness and strength are one and the same.

This way, power and vulnerability remain hand in hand without blame or fear. Those who are afraid are also afraid of being vulnerable. The most vulnerable are the strongest of all.

Those who are afraid are also afraid of power. The most powerful are the most vulnerable of all. With power and vulnerability as your allies, compassion runs closely behind, for you can see the vulnerability of others. There is therefore no desire to "make" others weak, for their weakness can be seen as equal to your own. How can you make someone else what they already are?

Equally, this is so with power. If another is powerful, you will rejoice in that power, for its presence is a breath of freshness and beauty. There is nothing to compete with. And in weakness and vulnerability, there is nothing to condemn.

Nobody can be powerful unless they control their own lives, and self-control results from the acceptance of responsibility. Nobody is to blame for your life or any aspect of it. You are responsible for everything you do, and this means *everything*—no exceptions. Once we understand this, we are powerful beyond any other—more powerful than the politician or the priest, more powerful than the president or the king—for we command every moment of our existence.

In this power, we comprehend vulnerability—just in the acceptance of our own power—for a lack of blame brings compassion toward ourselves, and compassion toward ourselves brings compassion for others, automatically, as if by magic.

We cannot make others powerful, only ourselves. And in this knowledge, we realize that we do not wish to make others vulnerable, but accept their vulnerability. We are all potentially powerful and all always vulnerable. Anyone who speaks of having a "thick skin" is merely a fool.

Remember—just holding someone's hands and smiling warmly at them is a creative act. Share power.

[15]

∎

Those who comprehend only fear retreat from the world. Those who comprehend power and nature grow out of that freedom. Therefore, allow those who fear to die fearing, allow those who comprehend nature to grow in freedom. Both of these preserve themselves and achieve complete victory. Do not identify, only accept with compassion.

Fear is learned. We are not born afraid. If we were born afraid, we would never leave the womb. Our parents, teachers, and friends teach us fear. We, in turn, if we do not learn differently, teach our young also to be afraid. This is the very source of all the wars in the world. War is born out of fear. Peace and joy are born out of love, balance, and, thereby, compassion. There is nothing mysterious about any of this. It is the simplest thing in the world—not esoteric or spiritual, just real.

The problem arises out of our addiction to fear. We love it. We cherish it. We also hate it and regret it.

This is addiction in its most powerful form, as it is re-asserted every second of every day. Worry is a misuse of imagination brought about by the addiction to fear. No more nor less than this.

The comprehension of individual responsibility—I am the only one that is responsible for my life—allows us to grow out of the freedom that results from it. But you cannot make others responsible, so leave them to their addiction. Leave them to their entrapment within themselves. You are not responsible for changing them. You are only responsible, naturally, for the compassion you will experience from your own freedom. Both the frightened and the free will achieve a victory of their own. You cannot help them. Identifying with either will not do more than destroy your own freedom. Simply accept with compassion. Acceptance is everything. If you do everything out of your own freedom, then every act is an offering at the altar of life. Thus speak to God.

[16]

■

The known is not worthy, the seen is not precious, the heard is not relevant—except through consciousness and love.

Until we have learned consciousness—in other words, awareness of ourselves—we will not truly know, see, or hear anything. When we are unconscious, all we know is what we have been taught, all we see is what we are identified with, and all we hear is that which we select through our suffering.

These things are not relevant except to our suffering and our fears.

Consciousness, a truly simple thing, opens the heart to life through freedom, opens the blind eye, and awakens the ear. It is as though, once conscious, we have been blind, deaf, and dumb until then. It comes as a great surprise to us that suddenly, all is clear for the first time, because up until that moment the blind eye of the ego has been the only sight we had.

Here is a great story to help us understand this truth. The Zen master Hakuin received a samurai warrior who had come to him for advice. A samurai is a great soldier, and this one was highly respected by all, even the emperor of the time.

He asked Hakuin: "Is there any hell, is there any heaven? If there is hell and heaven, where are the gates? Where do I enter from? How can I avoid hell and choose heaven?" He was a simple warrior, and he said, "I am a samurai, I am a leader of samurai. Even the emperor pays respect to me."

Hakuin laughed and said, "You, a samurai? You look like a beggar."

The samurai's pride was hurt, his ego damaged. He forgot what he had come for. He took out his sword and was just about to kill Hakuin. He forgot that he had come to this master to ask where the gates of heaven and hell are. Then Hakuin smiled and said, "This is the gate of hell. With this sword, this anger, this ego, here opens the gate." A warrior can understand this kind of reasoning. He understood at once: This is the gate. He put his sword back in its sheath. And Hakuin said, "Here opens the gate of heaven."

[17]

■

In ancient times, a peaceful warrior prevailed without force or effort. There is nothing clever or brave in a peaceful warrior. Though their campaigns are not luck; for they stand where the Way, and the Earth, supports them, while the unaware are always lost.

There is no kudos in consciousness. There is nothing special about being aware of yourself and of what therefore surrounds you. Consciousness is a natural process. The problem is only that human beings have forgotten it and therefore give it a special place. To those that become conscious, there is nothing special about it. No effort or force is required. Bravery is not the issue for a conscious, peaceful warrior. The evident bravery and awareness arise as issues only in the minds of the unconscious because they have no experience of these things; so identify and praise accordingly.

In any campaign for advancement, therefore, the conscious, peaceful warrior is not successful because of luck or happenstance but because in his awareness he will stand in the right place, at the right time, doing the right thing—simply because of his awareness of this place and time. Life, and the Earth, will support him in this.

The unconscious, in the meantime, are always lost, afraid, unhappy, suffering.

[18]

■

So it is that good warriors take their stand on all ground equally and observe all their surroundings with lively awareness, available to all opponents, all friends equally.

Therefore, a victorious army is aware that its heart is at war, and it accepts; a defeated army believes that it fights for peace, and it denies.

So for the conscious, peaceful warrior, all things are equal. Everything is in balance and filled with lively awareness, available to everyone, all of whom are ultimately friends.

The winning warrior knows that his heart can be naturally both at war and at peace. In our hearts and souls, we are equally at war and at peace once in balance.

But the loser believes that he is on a quest for peace—that this is somehow the only way. In this, he is in denial of war, and so loses.

The mind and the ego are constantly result-oriented. "If I do this, what will happen?" "If I spend this money, how much more will I make?" "If I meditate, what will I achieve?" Result-orientation is supported by the constant awareness of the shortness of time. I must keep fit, therefore I do an hour's exercise every morning at 8:00. I must meditate, therefore I do an hour's meditation at 7:00. This is nothing more than bad stress management, not good body management or spirit management.

Imagine that there are no predictable results. Imagine that results are always different and never consistent— that you never know what's actually going to happen as a result of what you do. Let's be honest, this is actually the truth. We only *hope* to know the future—we never actually know it.

Here is a story from the Zen tradition. Hyakujo called his monks together, as he wished to send one of them to open a new monastery. Placing a filled water jar on the ground, he said, "Who can say what this is without using its name?"

The chief monk, who expected to get the position, said, "No one can call it a wooden shoe."

Another monk said, "It's not a pond, because it can be carried." The cooking monk, who was standing nearby, kicked the jar over, and then walked away.

Hyakujo smiled and said, "The cooking monk becomes the master of the new monastery."

The ego plans, and whenever it plans it misses reality. Reality can only be encountered spontaneously; if you think about something beforehand, you may be ready but you will miss the truth. A ready person will miss; this is the contradiction. A person who is not ready, who has not planned anything, who acts spontaneously, reaches the very heart of reality.

[19]

■

Those who cultivate the Way do not need arms, and the rules keep themselves. Thus, governing is natural, and corruption is irrelevant.

Those who are in the Way—who know through conscious awareness the natural processes of life—do not need weapons of attack. The rules, through awareness of the Way, need no supervision, for nature dictates direction. In this way, those who govern do so through that nature, and corruption is a joke. Who can win through corruption that works beneath genius? To those who know its nature, it cannot be a threat, for it is no more than a kind of silliness.

Much of the problem with power and corruption is that, for the most part, both "power" and "corruption" are misinterpreted. We have mentioned the true nature of power—that it is gained only by responsibility, not by position. Corruption is defined according to the idea that too much power creates it—according to the famous statement by Lord Acton that power corrupts and absolute power corrupts absolutely. This gives us the impression that corruption is actually born out of power, where in fact it is not. Corruption exists within those that are already corrupt. They may be politicians or wealthy business men and women, but corruption is not created within them by their power. Power, or the illusion of it, simply gives already corrupted individuals the opportunity to express their corruption. Politics and business provide more opportunity for those that are already corrupt. And in effect, as far as our spiritual perspective is concerned, these individuals are simply fools, and those that fear them and either follow or attack them are fools also. Power is therefore simply a mirror for who the corrupt really are. If we develop our self-awareness and therefore our awareness of others, we will see the corrupt individual well before that person can do us any harm. In a society where self-awareness is the norm, corruption becomes irrelevant. In a society where there is little or no self-awareness, corruption is a serious problem.

[20]

■

The methods of the peaceful warrior are five—love, consciousness, vigilance, silence, and power. Relaxation and acceptance give rise to love, love and presence give rise to consciousness, consciousness gives rise to silence, silence gives rise to vigilance. Love, consciousness, vigilance, and silence give rise to power.

[21]

■

Therefore, a conscious group is like a pound compared to an ounce, a group in conflict is like an ounce compared to a pound.

When a peaceful man goes with others on campaigns as though they were together directing a massive flood into a deep abyss, this is a matter of formation.

A group of conscious individuals is an army unto itself, even if small in number, while a massive group of unconscious individuals is worth little. J. Krishnamurti, the spiritual teacher, said that if one hundred conscious individuals meditated together, even only on one occasion, the result would be a greater world consciousness.

Put the peaceful warrior at the head of the unconscious group, and much more will be achieved.

FORCE

[22]

∎

Force as a natural energy moves without effort. A warrior is forceful when in the Way, and burdened when not.

This is the fundamental difficulty of modern warfare, and the reason why all wars are lost. Force, such as that undertaken by flowing water, or turbulent wind, or the fire of a volcano, is moving with the natural balance of this peaceful planet—thus, it always prevails. The force of a modern human army, because it does not exist in balance and is not natural, always loses.

Even though a modern army may prevail to make temporary change, that change will never sustain, because both sides of the battle are unbalanced and have been created in order to sustain unnatural conditions. An army may intend to sustain a religious bias, or territorial greed. It may, as has been the case with terrorist attacks in the past, intend to enforce a point of view—a particular religious attitude perhaps—and the counterattacks undertaken by the other side's forces are intended only to do the same, but from a different point of view. Neither of these forces will sustain because neither has balance. They do not "walk in the Way." The terrorists act out of hatred, anger, stupidity, hubris, religion. This is without balance. The counter-attacking forces act out of similar notions—revenge, greed, fear, defense, etc. Here, too, there is no balance. Both sides are therefore losers, and nothing will be gained. No peace can be made out of war, and no unconscious battle can bring balance. God does not "save" either side in a war. To utter "God save America" or "Allah save Islam" is a worth-less wastage of breath. God will not save anything, for God is existence, and existence reflects only those that oc-cupy it. If those that occupy existence are unconscious, as is the case with any unconscious leader or army, the result will be nothing more than further war and destruction—utterly without any value.

The warrior who is outside the Way is burdened and will therefore only bring more war, unendingly. This is the case in most of the world today, and until consciousness and balance are achieved, it will continue to be so.

[23]

■

For power and strength to be effortlessly available, the warrior must discover emptiness and fullness. This is found through self-awareness, and the unexpected.

Therefore, the peaceful warrior knows the unorthodox infinitely through consciousness, which is as inexhaustible as a river. Consciousness is an everlasting cycle, born and reborn like the seasons.

Constant and natural power and strength—which bring the natural force of the wind or the sea—are found through the human comprehension of emptiness and fullness. This knowledge is the knowledge of balance in human nature. Humans do have the natural force of nature as much as the wind and the sea, but they must unlearn all that they have learned through society's largely misguided education.

Emptiness is the power of inner silence, which is

achieved through absorbing and following the five basic tenets outlined earlier in this book: love, awareness, vigilance, silence, and power. If any one of these five tenets is not practiced by the warrior, emptiness and fullness will not be achieved. Fullness is the power to accept change, even though it is unpredictable. Life is a journey, not a home. We are all travelers on a quest, and existence will offer us the unexpected at all times that we are open to absorb it and learn from it. This is true education.

The peaceful and powerful warrior therefore knows change and unorthodoxy as a friend. He or she knows it through the consciousness that derives from the practice of the five basic tenets. There are only moments in life, each moment being different. There is no pattern except the lack of a pattern. The mind attempts to make patterns and fails always. Thus, all modern armies lose, because they are peopled by dreamers.

[24]

■

The speed of rushing water, which has no anxiety, can move boulders without strain. The speed of a hawk brings the prey to give up its life naturally. So it is with the peaceful warrior, whose power and strength are calm and whose speed is natural.

The group or the individual that moves like rushing water moves without fear, and everything will fall in its wake. The group or the individual that hunts like the hawk will catch its prey without failure. The warrior, in order to find this natural force, must live consciously, calmly, and with a speed that is natural. He must accept who he is, not suppress it.

See the runner in his second breath. He has fallen into the Way and will never be tired. See the warrior that takes on his quest with consciousness. He will never fail and never be beaten, for these are not issues for him. No war is needed for such as they, for victory has occurred before the battle is met.

If a child is afraid in the dark, we say, "Don't be afraid, be brave." Why? The child is innocent, he naturally feels fear in the dark. We force him: "Be brave." So he also forces himself, then he becomes tense. Then he endures the darkness, but now with tension. Now his whole being is ready to tremble. This suppressed trembling will follow him his whole life. It was good to tremble in the darkness, there is nothing wrong with this. It was good to cry and run, nothing wrong with this. The child would have come out of darkness more experienced, more knowing. And he would have realized, if he passed through darkness trembling and crying and weeping, that there was nothing to fear. Suppressed, the child never experiences the thing in its totality, he never gains anything out of it. Wisdom comes through suffering and acceptance. Whatever the case, be at ease with it. It is, after all, who you are.

[25]

■

Order and disorder are a matter of self-precision, consciousness, and vig-
ilance and cannot be taken for granted, or timidity and weakness will arise.

For strength and power to be effortless depends upon synchronicity
with existence—a rock does not roll down a mountain because of the
rock but because of the mountain. The power and strength of the war-
rior are due not to the warrior but to his co-incidence with existence.

No individual or group can exist with natural force
simply because of outside training from an unconscious
teacher. The individual or group must learn self-precision,
consciousness, and vigilance in synchronicity with life.
These matters cannot be taken for granted, for they must
be sustained at every moment. The sustaining of every
moment begins only when the warrior recognizes the
present moment as the only important factor. Recognizing
the moment as the only important factor requires con-

sciousness and vigilance. This is the benevolent circle of existence.

The recognition of the moment includes the awareness of all that surrounds and exists within that moment. This vision of all that surrounds the moment exists through conscious awareness of what is in that moment—the air, the smells, the sights, the sounds, the feelings, the thoughts—all that exists in that moment. For the most part, we are taught to look outside ourselves, and our vision is hampered by the anxieties of our conditioning. If we fear our environment, then the environment will be tainted by the fear and only our blind eye will be open. Lose the fear and, magically, life becomes visible. Once life becomes visible, then we are in the Way and will automatically achieve awareness and power. This is synchronicity with existence. We are like rocks rolling down a hill. If we see the hill and feel how it carries us, or the river that flows beneath and around us, then we are conscious and powerful.

The most extraordinary thing about this "co-incidence" with life is that it works like magic. Accept the presence of fear through consciousness, and the matters that frighten us cease to do so. But there will always be another question, for God within us can never be known. Here is a beautiful poem from the twentieth-century Polish writer Leopold Staff:

I didn't believe,
Standing on the bank of a river
Which was wide and swift,
That I would cross that bridge
Plaited from thin, fragile reeds
Fastened with bast.
I walked delicately as a butterfly
And heavily as an elephant;
I walked surely as a dancer
And wavered as a blind man.
I didn't believe that I would cross that bridge,
And now that I am standing on the other side,
I don't believe I crossed it.

EMPTINESS
AND FULLNESS

[26]

■

Those who are first to confront themselves, awaiting the answers, will relax and love. Those who avoid self-awareness but blame will be exhausted and hate.

Hold close your self-responsibility. Confront your own doubts and be sure they belong only to you. This way, you are in control of all that counts for you—yourself and your needs. This way, you can relax because no one else is taking over your life. If you avoid yourself and look outward to others as being responsible for your problems or joys, then you drain your own energy and hate others for taking over your power, therefore hating yourself as well.

The great and eccentric, terrifying teacher George Gurdjieff once said:

Eventually, no matter what one starts with, one must go to Philadelphia. After Philadelphia all roads are the same.

Everyone must go to Philadelphia. Everyone thinks I mean American Philadelphia. But . . . to understand this, they must discover true meaning of "Philadelphia." Everyone must go to "City of Brotherly Love," then all roads are the same.

—SECRET TALKS WITH MR. G. BY E. J. GOLD

The original Philadelphia was one of the cities to which John of Zebedee sent letters at the beginning of the book of Revelation as told in the Bible. Philadelphia was named by a great king who loved his brother greatly and lost him during battle. Philadelphia was named as such because it means "brotherly love."

Gurdjieff simply meant that until we have compassion we are nothing, and that all roads, spiritual or otherwise, lead to that love.

[27]

■

Therefore, the peaceful warrior may draw inside and be available to others.

Others will come because they hope to learn, while those who are unconscious, those who are blind, will stay away, stubbornly unaware.

With this self-reliance, so you become available to life and to others who seek your wisdom. Those that sleep in their blindness will not seek you but will remain in their own unconscious worlds without resource.

God or wisdom is not invisible. We simply don't have the right sight to see. We are not attuned enough for the subtle to open its doors. The "organized" religions tell us that this world is available to us, and that heaven is not until we behave ourselves properly and then die. The world is "this," and heaven is "that." You must be dragged by death—from "this"—and then perhaps you will reach "that." They are seen as totally separate and dependent on our behavior in "this" life.

"This" and "that" are not divided. "This" reaches into "that," and "that" reaches into "this," once the blind eye of the ego is closed and your true sight is open. "This" is "that." This world is God. The visible hides the invisible.

Remain rooted in the earth, using the *chi* energy to ground you. Once grounded, you can reach for the sky.

[28]

■

So when those who come are confident, it is possible to move them further. When they are arrogant, it is possible to begin new lessons. When they are sleeping, it is possible to wake them up.

Therefore, the peaceful warrior hides where she cannot be found, disappears to where she is least expected.

The peaceful warrior will always become a teacher because consciousness, once learned, must give back to life. And the giving to life will invariably be giving back to unconscious beings. There is no pride in this, and the peaceful warrior will not seek out disciples but will be available to others when they seek wisdom.

This sutra simply defines the ways in which the peaceful, conscious warrior will form his or her position as far as being available is concerned.

Those that come to learn with confidence will be sent

deeper into their discoveries, while those that are overconfident will get shocks and new learning, too. Those that are asleep will be woken up. And to facilitate this design, the teacher will not easily be found—for if he is displayed, then he sets himself up as a superior. If he is hidden, then the unconscious one will have to work to find him.

All this is part of the modesty and gentility of the peaceful warrior. There is no manipulation, no format, and no demand. But also hidden in this sutra is the truth of where the true teacher resides—within each of us. We are always our own teachers, but perhaps we need a jolt in the right direction. In India, they call the true teacher "guru." This word has become corrupted by Western fears and attitudes, and by the presence, particularly in America, of false teachers and gurus.

The word "guru" is difficult to translate in a way that makes sense to a Western mind. The phenomenon of the guru is so deeply Indian that no other language of any country is truly capable of translating it effectively. The word "guru" is made of two words, "gu" and "ru." "Gu" means darkness and "ru" means one who dispels it. "Guru" literally means "the light." If you come across a Buddha or a Jesus, it will be of great help to you in finding your inner light, your guru, because upon seeing Buddha, a great enthusiasm and hope arises: "If it can happen to Buddha," who is just like you—the same body, the same bone—"if it can happen to this man, why not to me?" The hope is the beginning. Meeting with the master on the outside is the beginning of a great hope, a great aspiration, so all those who have found the inner light must, out of their resulting compassion, give the light to others in some way.

[29]

∎

Be subtle even to the point of being formless. Be mysterious, even to the point of being silent. Therefore, you mirror those who come to you.

For any teaching, the peaceful, conscious warrior must be the mirror—i.e., those that come to learn will see only themselves in the teacher. If the teacher is overburdened with character and ego, so those that come to learn will learn nothing except what they already know. This is the whole basis for all spiritual understanding. False teachers spread their egotistical wings and flap about in deception, while the truly enlightened are free of devices and transparent to all.

The true master will not fulfill your expectations, while a false teacher will tell you exactly what you want to hear. The latter will seduce you because he wants you to be his disciple and not leave him, because you, by following him, buttress his ego while he buttresses yours. This is of no value at all in any spiritual process or quest.

With the real master, you have to work hard, and it will be painful sometimes. The real master works on you as a sculptor, chiseling away at you. He takes you apart, chips away, in order to change your habits, to give you a new life. In a very true sense, the true master kills you, because he kills the ego. In effect, he is the source of your death, because only after death is there a chance for resurrection.

You can try this on your own, but it is much tougher, because then there's no one there to help you and give you some encouragement. You have no references, no guide, and the spiritual night gets very dark.

[30]

■

If you are one with yourself and those that come to you are each divided into many parts, you are concentrated and they are dispersed. Their disorder and chaos will strengthen your concentration.

These sutras can be seen as being concerned with teaching the unenlightened, or teaching yourself from within. They are also instructions on how best to deal with opponents in battle. If the general of the army is enlightened, so also his power to win the battle will be enlightened. Therefore, the enemy will suffer from their lack of power and their lack of enlightenment. This would mean victory without battle. If it were possible for leaders to employ enlightenment against their enemies, there would be no battle to meet. If it were possible for the so-called enemies to be enlightened, then there would never be any wars. Unfortu-

nately, neither modern leaders nor their enemies are enlightened, so war is inevitable and everlasting.

The great Indian teacher U. G. Krishnamurti said,
"Don't expect the world to ever be in harmony. If you were
able to take a time machine and go forward a thousand
years into the future, you would find the world still un-
harmonious. Nothing will ever change in this respect. So
you are left with only one alternative—your own harmony.
Be harmonious within yourself and you will easily concur
with the world. Then who cares what fools exist around
you?"

[31]

■

When the peaceful warrior remains mysterious and unknown, those that come will make many defenses. Many defenses mean small attacks.

Much ego does not mean good results.

So the peaceful and wise warrior is formless, mysterious, silent, and flexible—this is genius.

If you meet someone that is predictable—i.e., who you know immediately because he is like you—then dealing with him, making battle with him will be easy, and you can direct your arrows where they do the most damage. But if you meet the peaceful warrior, the enlightened being, he will not be so visible or predictable because he will maintain mystery. It will therefore always be necessary for the attacker or the pupil to fire many arrows in many different directions—small attacks. With the predictable, the ego is the only target, and we all know the ego because we all have one. With the peaceful warrior, there is no ego and therefore no target.

ON KNOWING
OURSELVES

[32]

■

Normally, in order to learn about ourselves, we amass our past experience and the wisdom of others. We then gather our inner strength and open to change. Nothing is more difficult than knowing ourselves.

The greatest difficulty in knowing ourselves is to turn the negative into the positive.

Therefore, make the effort vigilantly, expecting understanding. Once you reach the result sooner than you hoped, you know you have found the method. Therefore, self-knowledge is considered beneficial and exciting.

Here Sun-tzu outlines the way in which wisdom was ideally gathered in his time. The existing knowledge of ourselves is allied with new wisdom, and change takes place.

This is seldom the case today, as most of our experience and the teachings we receive lack wisdom and are largely peripheral—being involved in knowledge that is rarely enhancing to inner growth. We are not taught first to understand who we are, and if we don't know who we are, how can we know anything of any value? We may believe that we know this, but it is rarely true. All we are doing is projecting our personal prejudices onto any situation that comes along. This does not reflect inner knowledge.

Our education tends to be concerned with external factors that help us only in matters of finance or career and give us little to grow through. We are not taught to concentrate on our inner wealth of knowledge—on how our emotions work, how our instinct works, how our soul functions. These things remain buried by the ego and by the external information that society forces upon us. Our teachers are rarely wise, and so most individuals only pass through processes that give nothing beyond the average. When we react, for example, to external forces that make us angry or jealous or hurt, how can we effectively deal with these situations if we do not know who we are? We simply react in a "knee-jerk" fashion, and the situation is not solved.

Nothing is more difficult than knowing ourselves, and although many may claim self-knowledge, few achieve it in fact.

This external knowledge—science, mathematics, geography, history, politics, organized religion—provides nothing positive for inner growth. Most organized religions, for example, are life-negative because their very organization kills the spirit of the original religiousness, and therefore, they provide little for our growth toward positive joy. We do not know who Buddha was, we do not know who Jesus was. We know only what has been passed down by generations of prejudice and ignorance—by the priests who also know nothing about who they are and who have a private axe to grind. They tell us that they speak to God and are therefore qualified to speak to us. They know nothing of God, and so they give us only their version of madness.

Vigilance and positivity are essential factors in learning the new wisdom that is needed to become energized by life. We can know when we have found something essential to our inner growth by the fact that understanding arrives quickly—i.e., we comprehend the truth of our new discovery without great effort, which is another positive aspect of our hidden capability.

We use the external, objective knowledge that we receive from the outside world to benefit us by passing it on to others, to situations, to events, etc. This is essential, of course, for us to earn a living and to find an environment that at least gives us some sense that we might one day be secure, even if this is not true. Nothing wrong with this. The problem arises, though, when this kind of knowledge exists to the disadvantage of everything else. We are so preoccupied with our external knowledge—our money-making capability, our satisfaction in relationships, etc.—that the inner is totally neglected and forgotten. We care only about the outside and never about the inner wisdom and knowledge that have been neglected. It is, again, the whole reason why human beings are always at war, always grasping, always vengeful.

There is a kind of joke, told in the East, that gives us a lighter hearted version of this problem. A politician was bitten by a dog, and a few days later his doctor told him that the lab tests were positive, that the dog had rabies, and that he was infected.

The politician pulled out a notebook and began writing furiously.

"Wait, wait," said the doctor. "No need to start writing your will. You'll be okay—there is a cure for this."

"Forget about the will!" shouted the politician. "This is a list of the people I am going to bite."

He wants only one thing—to use his situation for the benefit of his ambition, leaving his own health second. This is so often our way in the modern world.

[33]

∎

Trying to do too much too quickly is not useful; yet to face only small aspects with short convenience brings poor results.

So if you undertake a marathon, using too much energy and enthusiasm, aiming too high, your ego will overcome, reinstating habits; the established unconscious will sustain; and the truths you wish not to face will remain hidden from you. Take one thing at a time, though do not outline too precisely. Keep your resources intact.

As always, Sun-tzu emphasizes the balances of life—the Way of the Tao. Undertaking too great and long an effort and expecting to achieve quickly does not produce good results. Equally, to deal with small aspects of growth and change with little patience is not going to bring good results. What arises out of these excesses is that the heart and soul become exhausted and the mind takes over with the ego, and we revert to form—existing habits become dominant once more. As such, prevailing habits overcome the likelihood of change for the better, and the old reinstates, hiding what we wish to avoid facing.

Only the resources of positivity and self-knowledge need to remain intact. Examine one aspect of yourself at a time, and do not analyze too closely. Analysis is an act of mathematics—privy only to the mind, and operated by the mind. So it is, as in all psychoanalysis—the thoughts examining the thoughts, a largely purposeless operation. The heart does not analyze but prevails, breaking out the specifics through a more subtle method than the mind knows.

We say that we have done "all the groups," "all the therapies," and that no result has been achieved. We think, therefore, that we are too deep for common therapies to prevail, but in truth we are merely operating from the mind. Our judgments of ourselves are simply negative, so naturally the result is going to be negative also. We have worked so hard and so quickly, going from group to group, to make change in ourselves, and nothing has worked. The ego tells us that this is because we are so deep, so complex, and we are proud of this. Whereas, in fact, all that has happened is that we have not done anything except boost the ego further as fast as we could. Our psychoanalysis took years, and where are we now? Our group therapies took more years, and where are we now? Nowhere, but we still have an intact ego. Actually, we have an ego that is stronger than it was years ago because none of the effort was undertaken with the right foundation. So we miss, and we miss, again and again, because we do not ask the right question, or we ask it from the wrong place—from the ego, not from the heart.

There is a wonderful story of a man who lived in a town that Buddha used to visit often. During forty years, Buddha always came there and spoke to people and listened to their questions. This one man, who was a trader with a store, would visit and sit before Buddha with all the many people around him, and then leave to go back to work. He never remained for more than a few minutes, and would then bow to Buddha and depart.

When asked by one of Buddha's closest disciples why he did this every time, the trader answered: "I have a business to attend to, and no one else can do it but me. Also, sometimes, there are relatives that visit, or my wife is sick." And this was always his story, every year that the Buddha came and spoke.

This man never stayed long enough to ask anything.

Eventually, after forty years, the Buddha was in the town and very old and ready to enter the final Samadhi (passing from the body into oneness with existence). At his talk one day, he announced to his disciples that he would now go to his final rest. Buddha spoke to his disciples, gathered around him: "Do you have anything to ask—because soon I will enter into the final Samadhi, the final ecstasy, and then I will not be able to come back and answer you." The disciples could not speak and had nothing more to ask as they sat in dismay at the passing of their master.

At that moment, the trader appeared and pushed his way through the monks to stand before Buddha: "I must see him. I have missed again and again all these years, but now I have a question to ask." Buddha opened his eyes and sat willing to answer this man's question, but the trader, at last, could not remember what he had intended to ask, and this was his last chance. "I cannot remember my question, but next time I will remember, next time I see you." And there was no next time, for Buddha died that day.

One of the greatest reasons why we in the Western world fail to ask the right question from the right place is the predominance of the Western ego. In the East, with the background of Hinduism or Jainism, the ego of the individual is brittle—easily cracked and broken—because the Eastern religions do not concentrate on the power and presence of the ego but rather on surrender to the master. If you are habitually conscious from childhood of the concept of surrender, then having your ego dismantled by a master is likely to be a simple affair. Results will more easily occur, because if we truly want to become enlightened or wise, at some point the ego must be smashed, and born out of that death is the truth and ultimate joy and balance available to us all.

But in Western religions, the ego is everything, and society emphasizes its importance, so to have an Eastern master attempt to crack that hard shell that surrounds you is difficult and painful, and may never work to release you. The ego is slightly damaged—cracked with a hairline fracture, but it remains intact, and the disciple returns from the master with little effect except resentment and suffering— thus hating the master, hating and resenting the "cult" or "religion" that caused such pain. This is particularly so in the U.S., where the ego is stronger than almost anywhere else in the world. So Americans generally fear cults as a result—are suspicious of them—and this gives rise to the worst forms of cult religions themselves—just to confirm their suspicions. It is all being done too fast and without the inner understanding of what it is intended to do. We are like arrows being fired into the air, at high speed, and without aim, without comprehension, thrashing about as a result of our wrongful conditioning, therefore causing the arrow to fall in the wrong place.

Take one thing at a time, though do not outline too precisely. Keep your resources intact.

[34]

∎

If you do not know who you are, you will not relate successfully. Unless you are willing to become familiar with yourself—your peculiarities, characteristics, eccentricities, you cannot begin the work of self-awareness. Unless you spend time listening to your own ways, you will not maneuver well in your own territory or the territory of others.

The simplest statement. If you do not know who you are, you cannot know who anyone else is. If we stand in a dark room, we can see neither ourselves nor anyone else. The moment light hits our presence in the room, it also hits the presence of all others near us. Light can only ever be achieved, in this respect, from within us.

There is an old analogy of the difference between the Western form of spiritual recognition and the Eastern form. It is like the difference between a man with a flashlight that has a narrow beam in a garden and a man with a suddenly floodlit garden. In the Christian, Western concept of spiritual discovery—learning this and learning that—we need a narrow-beamed, concentrated flashlight in our hands, and as we shine it on the flowers and the trees and the ground, we gradually discover what we want to know—step by step. It will be an arduous task, and knowing one thing, under the beam of the flashlight, will not necessarily tell us anything about the rest. Whereas, in the Eastern way of comprehension—Buddhism, Hinduism—the big, powerful light flashes once and takes in the whole garden in one big, dramatic flash. You see it all in context, in one moment, and then comprehension—enlightenment (literally)—is yours.

It is not to say that one method is better than the other. Within the Protestant ethic, we are taught that progress is all-important—that we should move from "here" to "there," and the sooner we get to "there," the better. This simply enhances the idea of progress as the be-all and end-all of perfection, which is not the subject of this book.

The big flashing light that displays everything in one great blast is the antithesis of the small flashlight beam that picks out each detail and results in a final revelation, perhaps. But if the sudden realization—the satori, the Zen approach—is the way we choose, it can happen at any moment. It does not require progress or practice. It does not require constant effort or determination. It requires only a moment in which it happens—without rationale, without purpose, without end—just a moment in the present. And this is anathema to Western thinking, because no thought is required—indeed, thought prevents. No progress is required—in order to find this instant change, we do not have to work, meditate, learn. We simply have to be present in the moment and open to whatever comes along.

[35]

∎

So a peaceful self-regard is established by inception, moved on by vigilance, and adapted through flexibility and understanding.

In order to find yourself and the truth about your being, and thereby establish joy in it, there must first be the desire to make it happen, then the determination and vigilance to continue it moment by moment. Once established as a new habit, always preserved and observed, it must be followed by flexibility and understanding. Flexibility arises from a willingness to accept change, even though it may not always be attractive; and understanding must arise from compassion—the willingness to accept who you are—even if it does not at first appear to be what you wish it to be. Remember also that vigilance is not determination or willpower, but a desire to sustain.

The magic of this is that existence coincides with your progress, and the moment that you accept yourself, you become perfectly as you would wish yourself to be. This is not a matter of ego, or self-aggrandizement, but is simple, uncomplicated truth.

[36]

∎

Therefore, when things are going well and fast, your work is like the wind. When it is slow and gentle, it is like the forest; it burns like fire, is solid as a mountain.

Your work will be mysterious. The movement of it will roll like thunder.

When discovering one familiar aspect of yourself, use the right tools. When opening up to other, broader aspects, reward yourself with success.

The process of self-discovery is ongoing. Whether we feel that we have reached an advanced state or simply an early beginning, the quest continues without completion. In fact, on the Way, we are never advanced, nor have we the likelihood of any completion. We are simply pilgrims on the road to nowhere. "Advanced" and "retarded" are merely concepts of the ego and mean nothing in terms of the joy of the soul to be traveling through the life of balance, joy, and inner peace.

For every step of this journey, we must use the right tools to help ourselves along—the tools of the five basic tenets that we have mentioned before: love (the Way), consciousness, vigilance, silence, and power. In some ways, vigilance is the most important, for we will quickly fall by the wayside if we do not retain our discipline—our joy at every step. In fact, with a simple trick, we can ensure this aspect of our journey. Each morning, there is a choice— joy or sadness. We can wake up in the morning from sleep, and there is always that choice: Shall I be happy or shall I be sad? If we allow the variances of our emotional moods and thoughts to dictate to us, then very often sadness or depression or doubt or fear will carry weight over joy. There are so many difficulties to choose from, after all. Our finances are not enough, our loved one doesn't satisfy us, our thoughts are depressing, our body is sick—so much to keep us on the low road! Choose your thoughts consciously. Find a good thought, find a good mood. It's as simple as that, and the choice for joy overcomes the identification with sadness.

Reward yourself with your successes, however small they may be. There's always one success to be found; choose that over failure, and the Way is recovered.

[37]

■

Retrench and meditate after each part of your work. Learn the measure of who you are, how far you can go—this is the best rule for self-assessment and discovery.

When you feel that you have found something new in your inner life—something that was not there before—stop, be still and silent. Find a calm place and time to sit in meditation, and go deeply while in that silence into what has happened. Feel it. Don't analyze it, just feel it. Feel the goodness and joy of it, and congratulate yourself with the healing of that wonderful silence and what has come out of it. Relish the joy of it, and keep the resulting sense of your own good progress in your heart. This emphasizes and confirms, within the body and soul, that which has been found.

But how to find silence? This is the tough part, for the

mind continually steps in and takes over the spaces that lie between thoughts. Thoughts come so fast; how can we reside in the space between them? The mind can never be silent, but we ask from the mind, and if we ask, "Where is silence?" then there is none, because the mind is doing the silence. It's a bit like asking where the rainbow is. There's no rainbow; it's an illusion, like the mind. The mind is simply a state of mind that ultimately causes all the problems. This is not to say that the mind has no purpose—actually, it is *all* purpose and has its uses, but finding silence is not one of them.

Chuang-tzu, one of the three most celebrated Taoists, once dreamed that he had become a butterfly. When he awoke, he was very depressed.

"What has happened?" people asked.

Chuang-tzu said, "I'm confused. During the night, I dreamed I was a butterfly."

His friends were puzzled as to why this should worry him.

Chuang-tzu said, "If I can become a butterfly in a dream, perhaps the butterfly dreams that she is Chuang-tzu."

So what's real? The truth is that we have become minds. We have not awoken into reality, because the mind has become everything. True awakening is awakening to no-mind.

When you awaken, you don't achieve an awakened state of mind, you achieve a no-state of mind, you achieve no-mind—the place of silence.

What does no-mind mean? This is a difficult question to answer, but sometimes, unknowingly, we are just sitting in an ordinary situation, not doing anything in particular, with no thought in the mind, for mind is no more than a series of thoughts. It isn't anything substantial, just a procession of thoughts, none of which means anything at all until we grab them and make something from them. Be aware of these moments where no thoughts are there—this is no-mind also.

But thoughts move so fast; how can you find an interval between them? But they're there for sure, and the more aware we become of these moments of no-thoughts, the more familiar they are and the easier to sustain. That interval is you. When the mind is not there, who are you? Chuang-tzu or the butterfly? Neither. And what is the state? Are you in an enlightened state of mind? If you think you are in an enlightened state of mind, this is, again, a thought; and when thought is there, you are not. If you feel that you are a Buddha, this is a thought. If you think you are sad, this is a thought; or happy, or bored, or depressed—all thoughts. The mind has entered, now the process is there; again the sky is clouded, the blueness lost.

[38]

■

Ancient wisdom tells us that in matters of ourselves and our ways, we are deaf and blind, so we must bang cymbals to hear, raise flags to see. Magnified sources bring initial awareness, for we are asleep and must be woken. Once the effort is unified and concentrated, do not allow stray thoughts, blind alleys, and irrelevant diversions. This is the rule for concentration of effort through vigilance.

The original story of the three monkeys that are deaf, dumb, and blind had a greater significance than the popular one we might remember. The monkeys were an allegory for humanity, which is not truly able to see, hear, or understand life to the full. We think we see, but we miss ninety percent of what is shown to us because we are so busy somewhere else—in the past or the future. We think we can hear, but there is so much more to sense than we find normally; and we think we understand, but we only understand through the mind, which has so limited a comprehension of life.

On a very basic level, for example, take the art of seeing. There is a great difference between *looking* for something and *seeing* in the true sense. Looking means you are looking for something; you already have some idea of what you're looking for. You come to a location and you are looking for a building or a person—you have an idea, a shape of what you're looking for. This looking is already prejudiced. If you are looking for God, you will never find Him because looking means you have a certain idea already of who God is. And your idea is bound to be either Christian or Judaic or Hindu or Mohammedan. Your idea is going to be your concept, and your concept can never be higher than you. It is, after all, *your* concept. Your concept is bound to be rooted in ignorance, borrowed. At the most, it is just belief; you have been conditioned for it. Then you go on looking for that thing.

A person who is looking for truth will never find it, because his eyes are already corrupted; he already has a fixed concept. He is not open. All interpretations will be according to an accepted idea of his own. He will miss the truth. A man who is looking for something will always miss it.

Seeing is just clarity—open eyes, open mind, open heart. Not looking for something in particular; just ready and receptive. Whatever happens, you will remain alert and receptive. You will be without preconception.

True seeing is naked. And you can come to truth only when you are absolutely naked; when you have discarded all clothes, all philosophies, all theologies, all religions; when you have dropped all that has been given to you; when you come empty-handed, not knowing in any way. When you come with knowledge, you come already corrupted. When you come in innocence, knowing that you don't know, then the doors are open. Only that person who has no knowledge is capable of knowing.

Once a seeker came to Bayazid, a Sufi mystic, and asked, "Master, I am a very angry person. Anger happens to me very easily; I become really mad and I do things. I can't even believe later on that I can do such things; I lose my senses. So, how can I drop this anger, how can I control it?"

Bayazid took the head of the disciple in his hands and looked into his eyes. The disciple became a little uneasy, and Bayazid said, "Where is that anger? I would like to see it."

The disciple laughed uneasily and said, "Right now, I'm not angry. But sometimes I am."

So Bayazid said, "That which happens sometimes cannot be your nature, but an accident. It comes and goes. Like the clouds—so why worry about the clouds? Think of the sky that is always there."

[39]

■

Keep your intentions clear before your senses; put up signs and re-minders to be vigilant, and practice both day and night.

Remove by this vigilance the sting of the ego, the power of your lazi-ness, and entrapment.

True vigilance is a constant art. You can never let go of it. You must keep yourself aware at all times, and the more you practice this, the easier it will become—but it is not the art of habit.

Vigilance is the opposite of habit, because the moment it becomes a habit, it ceases to be vigilance.

Vigilance is fresh, new, and absolutely different at all times, while habit is sleep, drowsiness, and boredom—automaton behavior.

So keep signs in your head, in your office, in your home, in every room—literally—to remind yourself to be conscious, because if you don't do this, habits will form, and all habits—except those that prevent you from physical damage—are bad habits. The conscious being has few habits. The conscious being is always awake, even when asleep.

By remaining always vigilant, you banish the ego and all its absurd habits; you banish laziness and entrapment in the habits that were born out of fear and doubt.

[40]

■

Be aware of the daily cycles of energy. The morning is always best for work, the middle of the day less good, and the evening least good. Choose your moments therefore—for body work and vigorous meditation, take the morning; for awareness of past conditioning and mental work, take the middle of the day; for meditation and spiritual work, take the evening. This way, you will master your energy cycles.

Most of us are already aware of this very basic piece of advice, but it is interesting that it appears in a text that has hitherto been thought of as simply a tactical war system. Sun-tzu considered all aspects of human frailty and power, and one of the most basic aspects is the functioning of the human body, and therefore the mind and spirit. Work on the body in the early part of the day because it is at its highest level of energy and strength at that time. For active meditations such as Kundalini or Dynamic meditations or running and jogging, use the early morning energy to bring calm and brightness to the body and mind—reducing the amount of anxiety and worry. Sitting on your backside attempting to be still and calm is probably going to be a worthless operation unless the body is able to exercise its power and energy. Most of us must go into stressful jobs and situations, and with no physical meditation such as those suggested above, the degree of anxiety and worry is merely increased; whereas if we have directed the body's high energy, we have a far better chance of being focused and unafraid during the morning.

The second recommendation is a bit less obvious—"for awareness of past conditioning and mental work, take the middle of the day." This is not intended as a psychoanalyst's dream!

The process of self-reflection is not a process of analysis, but a process of awareness. Memory and thought are needed to recall events in the past, perhaps, but not in order to dwell on them and identify with events that may have occurred decades ago—that is merely the mind working on the mind, and in any case, it is all in the present, with no relationship to the past at all, for there is no past. Meditate on today, on now, on this moment. Events from the past will occur. Let them be as they are. Do not analyze; accept them, like passing clouds. Be simply aware.

The difference between the meditator's method and the analyzer's method is cheese and chalk. The meditator is aware of memories and thoughts that remain in the mind from the past. These can be accessed either through present events that trigger their memory or through deliberate attempts to recall them. They are only of significance either because of some current situation that requires corroboration or "evidence," or because the past event somehow etched a painful "scar" on the mind and heart. The analyzer dwells on the event and identifies with it—i.e., relives it—while the meditator pays no attention to what effect it has on the mind and heart, but simply allows it to remain there untouched, paying attention to its effect on the heart and mind but ignoring this in favor of simple awareness of it. It's a bit like the difference between gluing something and allowing it to slide down a duck's back!

The meditator lets it slide, avoiding all glue! Why relive the past? You cannot anyway, because you are in the present, so the event will be different because you are different, and your memory is probably imperfect anyway. Ducks have it.

[41]

■

Keep your life always ordered and tidy, thus freeing the mind of anxiety concerning environment. Live calmly against chaos. This way, the heart remains at peace.

Simple advice—nothing else to say.

[42]

■

Spend time simply watching, in calm and stillness. Watch your secure times, your insecure times. Watch your power and your weakness. This way, you master your own strength and capability.

Remember that you have been living with familiar habits for many years—do not confront them too hard and fast. Be master of the flexible and the compassionate.

In many of the Eastern spiritual scriptures and writings, there is mention of the "Witness" or "Watcher." Behind this presence, which should not be associated with an identity, is the concept that we each have an aspect to our spiritual presence in the body that is essentially a witness to all that we do. The basis for this is that the witness is behind the body, the mind, the moods/emotions, and the spirit and is disassociated from them all. It is nevertheless within our capability to access this watcher of our lives and find that its presence is of great value.

Imagine that the body, the thoughts, the moods/ emotions are like passing clouds and you are sitting on a hill watching them go by. However powerful the clouds may be, however troubling or happy or difficult these clouds are, whatever amount of rain or shine they offer, you—as the Watcher—are unaffected. It is almost as though your own life is a projection on a screen, like a movie, and none of it has the slightest effect on you as it passes across your awareness. This is the Witness—this is meditation.

In Hinduism, there is a practical expression of this. Hindus believe that there is "heaven" and "hell," but there is also a third existence that they call "Moksha." Moksha is neither heaven nor hell but the absence of both, and Moksha is that which all Hindus aspire to. Heaven, for a Christian, is no more than desire, while hell is fear. Moksha is neither desire nor fear, but simply the presence of neither—i.e., pure silence and peace. Sun-tzu suggests that we watch both our secure feelings and our insecure feelings, our power and our weakness. If we allow these feelings to pass without identification, then we reach Moksha. In effect, we drop both sides of the coin and find pure gold instead.

■

Learn not to attack yourself; be gentle and patient with yourself. Be aware of the tender spots that are supported by much time and habit.

Be aware of your ego; it can be crafty and complex. Do not rush at yourself where boundaries are well established.

We have a habit of punishing ourselves for the things we feel are wrong or disturbing in our own psyches. This self-abuse, which takes many, sometimes-complex forms, is almost invariably some sort of self-defense. We also often lie about ourselves both to ourselves and to others, and these aspects of our conditioning may have been present and may have been abused by us for much of our lives.

There is a story of a disciple who lived in the ashram of a great master in the East, and she was married to a man to whom she had lied about a love affair. The husband went to the master and told him that he was jealous and felt angry at his wife for her infidelity, but that more than this, he felt deeply hurt that she had lied about it to him—that he had pestered and pestered her to get the truth but she would not tell him what had happened or why she had done it.

The master took the husband aside and told him to stop pestering his wife, that he knew of her infidelity and that was enough. She had stopped her affair and was now back with him and loving him again. "What more do you want?" the master asked him. "Her lies are her privilege. These details are her secret, and you must not expect to know everything about her. You cannot own another person. Her lies are to protect herself. Leave her alone with them, for they are like a secret treasure, and not knowing them does not detract from your loving each other."

We all tell lies, all the time. Mostly small and delicate things are protected by our lies, and we have every right to keep them secret, but those things that are so personal that we must cover them up should not be reason for us to abuse ourselves. Be tender with yourself, there is nothing wrong with you. The basic truth about all of us is that ultimately we are perfect as we are. Our judgments about ourselves are what make us judge others, and these prejudices are misguided, ALWAYS.

[44]

■

Be aware of your own and therefore others' poisons and tricks. Your ego is complex and vengeful. Do not position yourself in a four-walled box—leave always one wall down. Make allies and accept weaknesses. This is the beginning of the Way.

This remarkable sutra is one of the most beautiful and important in the whole of Sun-tzu's treatise. "Your ego is complex and vengeful. Do not position yourself in a four-walled box—leave always one wall down."

The human ego always wants to win a battle and therefore tends to want to trap the "enemy," which it sees as anyone who wishes to prevent it from progress of some kind. This strategy of entrapment occurs both to the "hunter" and to the "hunted." If we fail to be friendly and harmonious with ourselves and with others, we make only enemies, both of ourselves and of others. This is not the Way.

The Indian master U. G. Krishnamurti was asked a question by a disciple: "How can I change the world?"

His answer was simple but revolutionary: "If you are reborn a thousand years from now, the world will not have changed. It will still be chaotic and crazy. Change yourself and become harmonious with whatever the world is. In this way, you change the world of your perspective."

There is a story of a Zen monk who was deeply immersed in self-discovery. He had converted from being a Jesuit priest and so was accustomed to very harsh disciplines. The Zen master of the monastery in China, as always with Zen masters, rarely taught through word of mouth but almost always through action. He had not, in fact, spoken a single word to the monk since his arrival.

The Zen monk would meditate every day for hours and hours, and gradually he would take his times of silence farther and farther away from the other monks. Eventually, he went to a hut up in the nearby mountain and remained there day and night for a whole week, sitting constantly and hardly eating. The hut was ramshackled, so the monk built new walls made of mud and hay, with a tiny door on one side. The Zen master watched each day on his walks into the mountain, but said nothing to the monk. Eventually, one day, the Zen master took his walk and found that the monk had removed even the door and plastered it over, so that there was no way in or out of the hut.

The Zen master went up to the hut and kicked down one of the walls. He stood in the space that was left and whacked the startled Zen monk on the head with his stick. "Life is not afraid of you. Why are you afraid of it?" the Zen master said. The monk was so surprised to hear his master's voice that he left the hut immediately and meditated with the other monks in the fields about the monastery. He was seen often to laugh and joke after this event.

The spiritual life, indeed all life, is not esoteric. It is written on each leaf of each tree, on each pebble on the seashore; it is contained in each ray of the sun; whatever you come across is life in all its beauty. And life is not afraid of you, so why should it hide itself? In fact, most of us are hiding ourselves. We are closing ourselves off from life because we fear it. We fear to live, because life requires a constant death.

FLEXIBILITY

[45]

■

In the peaceful warrior, the heart and soul will direct the body and mind. The heart and soul of the wise avoid difficult terrain. The borders between heart and body must remain well established so that there is no isolation, only coincidence.

When out of coincidence, find coincidence first. When the terrain is not coinciding, begin again.

If I believe that life gives me nothing, then life will oblige. If I believe that nobody can be trusted, then life will bring me distrust. If I believe that I must fight to win, then life will bring me battles. If I am joyous, compassionate, and at peace, then life will coincide. Whatever I pray for, life will grant me, instantly.

In our lack of consciousness and the noise that occupies our minds and bodies, we most frequently find difficult terrain to walk upon. Our jobs make us stressed, our personal lives are filled with much anxiety. Many of us, of course, are so accustomed to this way of living that we do not notice the din and the pain. This, we think, is normal. But once we have some even slight experience of the coincidences of life, where for a few moments or even as long as a day, things seem to go perfectly well, a new prospect enters our beings and we begin on the path—the Way. "The heart and soul of the wise avoids difficult terrain." A new habit can engage, though always with the presence of vigilance, in which we realize that we can actually help life coincide with us—we can work toward this coincidence consciously—but the method is not a "method" as we normally know it. It is a matter of making ourselves available to the coincidence, which is the basic teaching of this book.

[46]

■

Not all ways are the Way. Not all love is relaxation. Not all power is empowering; not all silence is energizing; not all strength is vigilance. In your enthusiasm, do not attack; at your center, do not seek out change; standing on solid ground, do not dig; listening to the heart, do not think through.

The Way finds you, love gives you wings, power provides, silence arrives, vigilance demands.

The Japanese master Nan-in was visited by a professor of philosophy. Serving tea, Nan-in filled his visitor's cup, and kept pouring. The professor watched the overflow until he could restrain himself no longer: "Stop! The cup is overfull, no more will go in."

Nan-in said: "Like this cup, you are full of your own opinions and speculations. How can I show you Zen unless you first empty your cup?"

We have so many opinions, so many ideas, so much junk in our heads that has been put there by our education and our prejudices about life, ourselves, and others. There is such an overflow, like a blocked sewage pipe, that we cannot make ourselves available to life itself. We cannot coincide with the truth of our existence. Put simply, we are deaf, dumb, and blind to life, but life goes on providing. All we need to do is listen.

[47]

■

Even the best peaceful warrior, who knows where to stand his ground, knows also how to adapt his power and vigilance. Stability is lonely without flexibility.

The lonely warrior does not find new warriors. Separation brings suffering, occupation sets aside for later, the soul yearns for growth.

The ego always seeks isolation because then it cannot be criticized or troubled by interference from others and from the truth of life, which it does not wish to know. The search for wealth is an attempt to seek isolation. The religious zealot seeks isolation through the "special" knowledge of God. The expert seeks isolation through learning. The politician seeks isolation through the acquisition of power. All forms of stability create isolation because there is no flexibility in stability and security.

Share your knowledge, your discoveries, your power, your beauty, and your truth, and be prepared for these to change as a result.

This is not the same as solitariness. To be solitary is to be alone in joy—to heal from society, chaos, or sickness.

[48]

∎

Consider not one without the other. Benefit walks hand in hand with disadvantage. Joy carries, pain enlists.

Everything has its partner—there is no pleasure without pain, no love without hate, no strength without weakness, no power without collapse, no anger without shame—they are partners, not opposites. We think always that we can have one without the other because we enjoy one and we dislike the other. We also think that we would like to be happier or more certain instead of sad or doubting. In truth, if we know that something is a partner with what we see as its opposite, we can let them both go. There is no need to be doubtful or certain, happy or sad. We can simply *be.*

[49]

■

The peaceful warrior expects no opposition and is therefore not disappointed.

Taken from the viewpoint of the most commonly interpreted translations of *The Art of War*, this would simply be interpreted as something referring to dominance: "The great warrior doesn't worry about opposition because he knows he can win." But perhaps there is a different way to see it.

The peaceful warrior expects no opposition because opposition is not an issue for him. What we pray for is always granted. If we expect opposition, battle, and conflict, then life will give us battles. If we coincide with life's natural patterns—with the Way—then conflict and opposition simply disappear. Why would I want to oppose myself? Absurd! So why would the opposition of others be of any relevance? No disappointment here, because even if someone stands up against me with what they may think of as opposition, I am not concerned. I will not coincide with this.

[50]

■

Be aware that when looking in, you will discover the following devices in the castle of the ego—sacrifice gives residence to collapse, over-exuberance brings avoidance to change, anger will not give up shame, purity is the mother of corruption, determination to love brings only suffering. Campaigns will fail if these five methods prevail.

There is a Japanese doll called the "Daruma" doll. This doll has a very heavy base, and however it is thrown, it always reasserts its base and ends up sitting upright. You cannot make it lie on its side or upside down. It always ends sitting upward. "Daruma" is the Japanese for Bodhidharma, the Buddhist who brought Zen from India to China (where it was called "Chan," and much later went to Japan to become Zen). The Daruma doll exemplifies the ego. All spiritual masters must face the Daruma doll because all unenlightened human beings, all disciples, are bottom-heavy—unable to sit anyway except with the ego uppermost. However hard you kick the ego, it will retain its position in control of the being.

In this sutra, Sun-tzu gives us specific examples of what the presence of the ego, always bouncing back into control, will do to the individual's view of life. Sacrificing ourselves for others or for situations outside ourselves will cause us eventually to collapse. Too much energy put into any one situation or person will prevent us from changing our habits. Anger always produces shame and guilt. Purity always brings corruption because no one can ever be pure—thus the madness of religious fundamentalism. Determination to love brings only suffering. Any campaign to learn about our truth and ourselves will fail if these "methods" prevail. The Daruma doll needs to fall over before we can progress.

CONTACT

[51]

■

In contact with others, the peaceful warrior first cares for herself. Be well in your body and mind, strong in your spirit.

Don't overreach yourself in efforts to care or teach—you are what you are, no more, no less.

The world is a little crazy. Parents and teachers try to teach children to love others. Mothers tell their children, "I am your mother, love me"—as if the child must force the love into existence just because the mother says so. The husband tells the wife, "I am your husband, love me"—as if love is a duty, as if love is something that can be done. Nothing can be done in these conditions except to pretend love, and once we learn how to pretend love, we have missed the truth of it altogether. Then we smile and pretend; laugh and pretend, and everything is false. And in the spiritual world, we will sit silently and pretend, meditate and pretend. Pretension becomes the style of our lives.

Drop, with practice, all the pretensions, and the real will be waiting there to explode. Don't listen to what others are saying, because that's how we learned to pretend in the first place.

Love is not a logical thing, and teaching others to do anything that is purely logical does immense harm to them, making life into a duty rather than letting it be a celebration. Life as a duty can never be a celebration, because you cannot laugh. Duty is merely a burden to be carried, but if we understand it, we can drop it.

Meditation, or any other potential for change, is just a situation; by meditating, silence is not going to be the automatic consequence. Meditation just creates the soil, the surrounding—preparing the ground. Meditation doesn't lead you to silence; meditation only creates the situation in which the silence can happen. Love doesn't automatically arrive with relationship. Relationship creates the ground in which you can love, but you need to have the love within you. It does not happen through being told to love. Love first yourself. The rest follows.

[52]

∎

Don't try to save the drowning. Let them who flounder sink; you do not know their needs. Adapt only to those that swim toward you.

There is a story of a man sitting near the Ganges in Allahabad, and it was just as the sun was setting and the day was over. Another man shouted from the water, "Save me! Save me!"

The man sitting by the river was not interested in saving anybody—he was too tired. So he looked around hoping that someone else would do the job of saving the drowning man. But there was nobody there, so finally he had to jump. And with difficulty, for this drowning man was heavy and fat.

Somehow he pulled him out, but the drowning man was very angry—"Why did you pull me out?"

The man who saved him said, "You were asking for help; you were shouting for me to save you."

The fat man said, "I was just afraid of dying, but I intended to commit suicide."

The savior said, "I am sorry, I had no idea that you were committing suicide."

So he pushed the man back! And the man started shouting again, "Help!"

The man on the shore said, "You can wait for somebody else to come. I will sit here and watch you commit suicide."

The drowning man said, "What kind of man are you? I am dying!"

The other man said, "Die! That's your business!"

How do you know what is happening to the person who lies by the roadside? This is the Eastern way—let them die. But in the West it's different because in the West there isn't so much poverty, and also there is little belief in karma, so it becomes clear that for this sutra to have relevance to the Western mind, it must also have something more subtle. For this sutra is about wanting to change ourselves through some deliberate method. It is about those that swim toward us, seeking change, seeking to be saved. Pay no attention, therefore, to the preacher or the fundamentalist in yourself. Pay no attention to your inner savior that attempts to drag you from the water. This is the ego, and it will not save anything. We are on one "pathless path" to self-acceptance. No Protestant ethic or Christian quest will help us in that.

[53]

■

Remain in your own power and silence. Allow your own love to stay intact. Never struggle against the flow, but allow the current to carry you and those who come along.

Solitariness is a healing force. Whenever you feel that you are interfered with or that your feelings hurt, don't try to solve the problem where you are, amidst many people and activities. Move away from society for a few days or even just a few hours, and remain silent, just watching yourself, feeling yourself, just being with yourself, and you will find a great force available to you that heals. In parts of the East, people go to the mountains or forests or someplace where they can be alone for a period, where there is nobody else to be bothered with. This aloneness provides better opportunity to see inside what is happening to you. The origin of the holiday (holy-day) was just for this purpose—to give people the chance to get away from the buzz and noise of everyday life and go to a place where they could find solitude and peace. We still search for the remote island to occupy our vacations for this very same reason, though there is often not much holiness available!

Nobody is responsible for you except yourself. If you are having a difficult time, you are the only one who can sort it out: It is your doing, after all. The Hindus say that whatever you are, it is your own work; nobody else is responsible for you.

If you can just be quiet, living with yourself for a few days, things settle automatically, because an unsettled state is not natural and will not last for long. It needs effort to prolong it. Simply relax and let things be, and watch, and make no effort to change anything. This is not to say that you have to do anything once you are in solitude. The "doing" is what happens in your normal life, and all this does is add to the confusion. Like a flowing river, the mud settles, the dead leaves go to the sea; little by little, the river becomes clean and pure.

[54]

∎

Keep your body and mind strong and healthy, especially when dealing with others. Eat well, sleep well, exercise well, but none of these excessively. Never permit sickness to plague you when dealing with others, for this will damage your center and your power.

In situations of negativity and suffering, keep the lightness of your life before you. Stay positive; this is your moment and your place—you can give only what you are.

Sun-tzu held great importance to the concept of leadership. He held that there are just a very few individuals who are capable of teaching and leading others. Unlike modern leaders, who have little or no basis in silence and meditation but do their work out of chaos and stress, Suntzu's leaders were wise beings, and his advice extended to the processes of self-awareness and inner beauty. What a different world it would be today if such beings were in charge of politics and international or national affairs. Sadly, this is unlikely to be the case in the near future. We, as a species, have encouraged the presence of largely greedy and troubled individuals to lead us. This arises, of course, because we ourselves lack any of the wisdom needed to choose the best leaders. What we are, so we choose.

Sun-tzu, by contrast, concentrates his advice on very personal, inner qualities such as exercise for the body, health of the mind, and a strong center to move out from.

[55]

∎

In situations of great trouble—of conflict, pain in others, and suffer-ing around you—wait in silence, bring yourself to your own center, then enter the field.

When life or situations are difficult, always go first back to your own center, and act from there. You, as an evolved being, can best respond to crisis from the one and only space that is certain—yourself, your inner seed.

For a small plant, the whole world is a potential crisis; there are a thousand-and-one risks. For the seed, there is no danger. The seed is imprisoned—protected. The seed is hard and secure, while the plant is fragile and soft and can be destroyed very easily. The flower is still more fragile—as fragile as a poem. The fragrance of the flower is still more fragile, so much so that it disappears. All growth is toward the unknown, toward the soft and fragile, toward the indefinable, so when you face crisis, sink back into the center—the seed of your existence—because from here you can act with confidence.

[56]

■

Be aware that there will be tricksters and pitfalls along the way. Your trust in life and in those around you must also contain understanding of distrust, fraud, manipulation, and danger. Wisdom is the spouse of innocence. Maturity is the brother of compassion. The beautiful forest is filled with thorns.

The world is a beautiful place
To be born into,
If you don't mind happiness
Not always being
So very much fun,
If you don't mind a touch of hell
Now and then
Just when everything is fine—
Because even in heaven
They don't sing
All the time.

This sutra and the one following are about deceit and trickery. Sun-tzu warns the peaceful, conscious warrior of the ways of the world, and how false people can be. What is most fascinating is the categories he chooses.

[57]

∎

You will find those who appear silent and still. You will meet those who appear sophisticated and powerful. They will draw you in for your wisdom and genuine strength, for your talent and ability, for your love and vigilance. Be aware that they draw you in to their advantage, for their gain.

You will find those who constantly change their position. You will meet those who drop feints and diversions before you.

You will find those who throw up sidetracks to confuse you. You will meet those who cause many distractions to attract you toward them. These people will kick up dust, cause smoke and mirrors to entice you. They will make stands and put down roots to make you falsely stable.

There will be those who will speak softly but attack harshly. There will be those who will wave big sticks and yet run away.

There will be those who appear gentle but seek to harm you. Those who approach you without wisdom and compassion are seeking to gain advantage from you.

Those who parade their knowledge before you are defending their weaknesses.

Those who bring only a small wisdom and remain secretive are trying to make you foolish.

The following lines are from Buddha's Dhammapada—the closest thing to a scripture that the Buddhist has:

We are what we think.
All that we are arises with our thoughts.
With our thoughts we make the world.
Speak or act with an impure mind
And trouble will follow you
As the wheel follows the ox that draws the cart.
Your life is determined by the nature of mind.
A disturbed mind creates a miserable life.
Suffering follows this mind
like the cart behind a horse.
A silent mind creates a peaceful life.
Happiness will follow this mind
like an ever-present shadow.
Living in the confusion of a disturbed mind
The false is mistaken for the truth
and the truth for the false.
Living in awareness with a silent mind
You will arrive at truth

and easily recognize the false as false.
Hate never yet dispelled hate.
Only love dispels hate.
This is the law,
Ancient and inexhaustible.
If a man's thoughts are muddy,
If he is reckless and full of deceit,
How can he wear the yellow robe?
Whoever is master of his own nature,
Bright, clear, and true,
He may indeed wear the yellow robe.

The "yellow robe" is the garment that was worn by all Buddhist monks during the time of the Buddha. It is still worn today.

Sun-tzu's sutras in this "Contact" section are a two-edged sword, for they refer both to the unconscious and the conscious individual in a variety of forms. They refer also to the potential for the downfall of the peaceful, conscious warrior who may be taken in by deceit and falsehood. But they carry much greater significance than this, and the piece quoted from the Dhammapada will help us appreciate the depth of what Sun-tzu has said in this section.

These sutras and the words of Buddha are about lies.

Buddha was not fundamentally interested in the outside world, for this was not his task. He was slightly interested in the mind and its methods, because in order to teach his disciples it was necessary for him to come to them at a level that they were familiar with—the thoughts. His greatest interest was in the innermost aspect of the human being—the heart and soul of all of us. The same can be said of Sun-tzu, although many translations of his work do not emphasize this but have been taken to be largely concerned with the outer realm, the subjective aspects of our existence: war, strategy, terrain, etc. This is only because the human, and particularly the male human, is almost invariably only interested in this aspect.

We are tremendously concerned with lies. Truth frightens us so much that we want to escape from it. Lies are that escape—escaping into a dream world that supports the ego. Dreams keep us temporarily happy, but they are constantly followed by frustration because they are never fulfilled. We make further dreams to compensate for the failure of the last dream, in which we even say to ourselves and others that our dreams come true. In truth, they never come true, because the present, when reached, is never as the future predicted it would be. How can it be? We continue to create new lies once the old lies have failed, so we invent new lies. Lies can be invented after all, while truth can never be invented. Truth *is*. Truth is found, not created. Lies are created, not found.

The mind feels good when it creates lies because the mind is the creator. And as the mind becomes the creator, so the ego is built. In truth, there is nothing to do; and as there is nothing to do, so the mind stops; and as the mind ceases its constant chatter, so it evaporates. And this is the reason why we must lie all the time, dream all the time, and therefore stay out of the present where the truth exists. Simple enough but very hard to do.

Within Eastern spiritual understanding, the world is illusory *(maya)*, but the world that Easterners refer to *(samsara)* is not the objective world, not the world of facts and science, trees and flowers, etc., but is rather the world that is weaved inside the mind. And it is this world that Sun-tzu often concerns himself with throughout the sutras of his text, and particularly in this section, which is concerned with the lies that surround the peaceful warrior and attempt to drag him back into unconsciousness.

Imagine that all thoughts stopped. Who then are you? There is, of course, no answer, for if the thoughts have left you, how can you answer with your name, your identity? All thoughts have stopped. All language has disappeared, even the words you use to relate to your country of origin, your home, your life. What you have become is nothingness. Buddha uses the word "no-self"—*anatma.* In such a moment, which incidentally is entirely achievable, you become egoless and simply a mirror of existence in bliss.

So when Buddha speaks of the "impure mind" and when Sun-tzu refers to those that are "sophisticated and powerful" and those that constantly "change their position," they refer to the presence of the mind itself, which is always in that sense impure because it exists in a dream world of lies, and the lies drag the peaceful warrior back to his mind and the unreality that forces him to lose consciousness. Misery will follow the impure mind, for misery is the product of the mind. Speak with the pure mind, and happiness will follow you—unshakably.

Remember Sun-tzu's five basic tenets—the Way (love), consciousness (heaven on Earth), vigilance, silence, and power. The peaceful warrior must sustain these tenets at all times, and there will be many opportunities to lose them through the deceits of the objective world.

ENERGY

[58]

■

There are five effective uses of energy—energy for yourself, energy for others, energy received, energy for long-life sustaining, and energy that protects against danger.

The sustaining and gaining of energy must have a foundation, requiring certain tools. There are appropriate times for using energy effectively—when the conditions are right.

Generally, when energy is needed, it is important to respond quickly to that need. When the energy is required within the body and mind, responses must come from understanding. If the body and mind are calm when inner energy is needed, there is no need to act. When the energy rises high in its degree and great heat is reached, be alert to it—assess the need for attention, make use of it if possible, remain still within it if not.

As always, pragmatic and to the point, Sun-tzu begins this sutra with the five ways that energy is of use. We commonly think of energy only in one form—as something we need to keep us moving. The Eastern teachers also see energy in one form, used for many different purposes such as desire or compassion. It is said by Buddha that only when desire is gone from the body can compassion occur. If there is desire—for possessions, for sex, for fear, for work, etc.—then one can never be compassionate. The same energy is used for different forms.

But where does this energy come from? Is it the beating of the heart and the consumption of food and drink? Is it from the sun and the wind? Does it arise from the heat of the body or the health and strength of the individual? If it is from the heart and the stomach, why is it then that some people have strong hearts and fat stomachs and no energy? Why is it that some people run great races with great energy and die young? There seems to be no rule about the energy available.

Jesus told a story—he repeated it several times in his teachings. Once it happened that a very rich man needed some laborers in his garden to work, so he sent a man to the marketplace. All the laborers who were available were called, and they started working in the garden. Then others heard, and they came in the afternoon. Then others heard, and they came just when the sun was setting. But the rich man employed them. And when the sun went down, he gathered all of them and paid them equally.

Obviously, those who had come in the morning became disappointed, and said, "What injustice! What type of injustice is this? What are you doing? We came in the morning and we worked the whole day, and these fellows came in the afternoon; just for two hours they worked. And a few have just come; they have not worked at all. This is injustice!"

The rich man laughed and said, "Don't think of others. Whatever I have given to you, is it not enough?"

They said, "It is more than enough, but it is injustice. Why are these people getting the same as us, when they have just arrived?"

The rich man said, "I give to them because I have got too much; out of my abundance I give to them. You need not be worried about this. You have got more than you expected, so don't compare. I am not giving to them because of their work, I am giving to them because I have got too much . . . out of my abundance."

Some work very hard to achieve the divine, some come just in the afternoon, and some come when the sun is setting, and they all get the same divine.

We all receive energy from the world, the universe. Our bodies receive it and distribute it according to their individual capabilities, but it all comes from the same source.

ACKNOWLEDGMENTS

I would like to thank my masters, who shall remain invisible; my wonderful wife, Manuela; my editor Mitch Horowitz for his sensitivity; Jeremy Tarcher for helping to make this happen; and my great friend David Patten.

ABOUT THE AUTHOR

Philip Dunn underwent the traditional English education until he reached his teens, when, through a series of twists of fate, he found himself in Tibet. During these teen years, he trained in the arts of Chou-lyn under the profound tutelage of a Tibetan master within the tradition of this ancient culture. The work in Tibet that he experienced was more than simply a physical training and included some of the most ancient and powerful rituals and spiritual teachings, from a man who brought his pupils to a high level of awareness and inner self-reliance. The terrain was rough and entirely alien to this young Western disciple, and it changed his life forever, bringing a consciousness of the warrior lifestyle that could never have been found in any Western tradition.

During the following years, he returned to Europe and trained further with a Chinese master in London, where he advanced to become a teacher himself. During this time, he also spent several years in India, where he met some of the greatest spiritual teachers of this century and advanced his understanding of the potential peaceful nature of humanity, becoming himself a more peaceful warrior, a lifelong student of ways of understanding human existence from an Eastern perspective.

This lifetime of learning and comprehending what he calls

"masked nature" is brought together in this entirely original inter-pretation of *The Art of War* as *The Art of Peace*.

Philip Dunn has also been responsible for the authorship of more than 40 books on various subjects within the spiritual category, and the creation of more than 500 books as a publisher.